TypeScript Unleashed

Strong Typing, Scalable Code, and Smarter JS Projects—Made Simple

Booker Blunt

Rafael Sanders

Miguel Farmer

Boozman Richard

Chapter 1: Getting Started with TypeScript

1.1 What TypeScript is and Why It Matters

1.2 Installing the TypeScript Compiler

1.3 Setting Up Your First `tsconfig.json`

1.4 Basic Types: string, number, boolean, arrays, tuples, and type inference

1.5 Hands-on: Converting a Small JavaScript Snippet to TypeScript

1.6 Compilation Process

1.7 Inspecting the Output

Chapter 2: Defining Interfaces and Type Aliases

2.1 Distinguishing Interface vs Type

2.2 Optional and Readonly Properties, Index Signatures

2.3 Union, Intersection, and Literal Types

2.4 Hands-On: Building a Type-Safe Configuration Loader

Conclusion

Chapter 3: Mastering Generics

3.1 Introduction to Generics

3.2 Generic Functions

3.3 Generic Classes

3.4 Generic Constraints

3.5 Utility Types: Partial, Pick, Record, and More

3.6 Custom Mapped Types

3.7 Conditional Types

3.8 Hands-On Project: Creating a Reusable Generic Data Service

Conclusion

Chapter 4: Object-Oriented Patterns in TypeScript

4.1 Introduction to Object-Oriented Programming (OOP)

4.2 Classes in TypeScript

4.3 Inheritance in TypeScript

4.4 Abstract Classes and the `abstract` Keyword

4.5 Implementing Interfaces in TypeScript

4.6 Access Modifiers and Parameter Properties

4.7 Mixins and Decorators Overview

4.8 Hands-On Project: Designing a Plugin Framework

Conclusion

Chapter 5: Managing Asynchronous Code

5.1 Introduction to Asynchronous Programming

5.2 Promises vs async/await

5.3 Error Handling Patterns and Custom Error Types

5.4 Intro to RxJS and Observables

5.5 Hands-On Project: Typed Data-Fetch Module with Exponential Backoff

Conclusion

Chapter 6: Tooling, Linting, and Formatting

6.1 Introduction to Tooling in TypeScript Development

6.2 Crafting a Solid `tsconfig.json` for Different Targets

6.3 Setting Up ESLint with TypeScript Rules and Prettier

6.4 Automating Builds and Type Checks in Your Editor

6.5 Hands-On: Configure a GitHub Actions Workflow

Conclusion

Chapter 7: Testing Strategies for Type Safety

7.1 Introduction to Testing in TypeScript

7.2 Choosing a Test Runner

7.3 Writing Type-Aware Tests

7.4 Snapshot Testing and Testing Async Code

7.5 Hands-On: Building a Test Suite for a REST Client

Conclusion

Chapter 8: Integrating with Frontend Frameworks

8.1 Introduction to Integrating TypeScript with Frontend Frameworks

8.2 React: Props, State, Hooks, and Context in TypeScript

8.3 Angular: Strict Templates and Dependency Injection with TypeScript

8.4 Vue and Svelte: Basics with TypeScript

8.5 Hands-On: Developing a React Component Library with Typed Props

Conclusion

Chapter 9: Building Typed Backends with Node.js

9.1 Introduction to Backend Development with TypeScript

9.2 Express and Koa with Decorator-Based Routing

9.3 Typing Request Payloads and Responses

9.4 Data Validation with Zod or Yup

9.5 Hands-On: Creating a CRUD API Server with Typed DTOs and Data Validation

Conclusion

Chapter 10: Working with Datastores and APIs

10.1 Introduction to Working with Datastores and APIs

10.2 Using ORMs for SQL and NoSQL Databases

10.3 Generating TypeScript Types from OpenAPI or GraphQL Schemas

10.4 Consuming Third-Party REST and GraphQL Services

10.5 Hands-On: Auto-Generate Types from an OpenAPI Spec

Conclusion

Chapter 11: Organizing Large-Scale Codebases

11.1 Introduction to Large-Scale Codebases in TypeScript

11.2 Project References, Path Aliases, and Composite Projects

11.3 Monorepo Setups with Yarn Workspaces or pnpm

11.4 Sharing Types and Utilities Across Packages

11.5 Hands-On: Setting Up a Two-Package Monorepo

Conclusion

Chapter 12: Packaging and Publishing Libraries

12.1 Introduction to Packaging and Publishing Libraries

12.2 Bundling with Rollup or Webpack for ES and CJS Outputs

12.3 Generating and Distributing .d.ts Declaration Files

12.4 Semantic Versioning and Changelog Automation

12.5 Hands-On: Publish a Small Utility Library to npm

Conclusion

Chapter 13: Optimizing Bundle Size and Performance

13.1 Introduction to Bundle Size and Performance

13.2 Tree Shaking, Code Splitting, and Lazy Loading

13.3 Analyzing Bundle Contents with Source Map Explorer

13.4 Fine-Tuning Webpack/Rollup Settings

13.5 Hands-On: Profiling a Demo App's Bundle Size

Conclusion

Chapter 14: Designing Scalable Microservices

14.1 Introduction to Microservices Architecture

14.2 Breaking a System into Typed Services

14.3 Communicating Between Microservices

14.4 Containerizing Services with Docker and Orchestrating with Kubernetes

14.5 Hands-On: Containerize a TypeScript Microservice and Test Inter-Service Calls

Conclusion

Chapter 15: Capstone: Full-Stack TypeScript Application

15.1 Introduction to Building Full-Stack Applications with TypeScript

15.2 Putting All Pieces Together: Frontend, Backend, and Services

15.3 CI/CD Pipeline, Monitoring, and Logging

15.4 Best Practices for Maintenance and Future Growth

Conclusion

How to Scan a Barcode to Get a Repository

1. **Install a QR/Barcode Scanner** – Ensure you have a barcode or QR code scanner app installed on your smartphone or use a built-in scanner in **GitHub, GitLab, or Bitbucket.**

2. **Open the Scanner** – Launch the scanner app and grant necessary camera permissions.

3. **Scan the Barcode** – Align the barcode within the scanning frame. The scanner will automatically detect and process it.

4. **Follow the Link** – The scanned result will display a **URL to the repository**. Tap the link to open it in your web browser or Git client.

5. **Clone the Repository** – Use **Git clone** with the provided URL to download the repository to your local machine.

Chapter 1: Getting Started with TypeScript

1.1 What TypeScript is and Why It Matters

TypeScript is a **superset** of JavaScript, meaning that it includes all the features of JavaScript while adding additional capabilities that help developers write more reliable and maintainable code. The most notable feature of TypeScript is **static typing**, which allows developers to specify what type of data their variables should hold, making the code less prone to errors.

Why Does This Matter?

JavaScript is a **dynamic** language, which means that variables can hold values of any type (strings, numbers, booleans, etc.). While this flexibility is great, it can lead to unpredictable behavior, especially in large codebases. Mistyped variables, unexpected values, and runtime errors are common in JavaScript. TypeScript eliminates these issues by enforcing type checks **at compile-time**, before the code even runs.

Imagine you're working on a large-scale application with hundreds of functions and variables. With TypeScript, you can specify exactly what type each variable should be, reducing the chance of bugs that might otherwise appear at runtime. This also helps other developers (or even you) understand the structure and intent of your code more easily.

By using TypeScript, you'll be able to:

- Catch errors earlier in the development process.
- Have better code completion and editor support.
- Write cleaner and more readable code, especially in large projects.

- Benefit from the features of JavaScript, with additional improvements.

1.2 Installing the TypeScript Compiler

To start working with TypeScript, the first thing you need to do is install the TypeScript compiler. TypeScript code needs to be **compiled** into JavaScript before it can be run in a browser or on a server (via Node.js). This is where the **TypeScript compiler** comes in.

Step-by-Step Guide to Installing TypeScript

1. **Install Node.js**
   If you haven't already, you'll need to install Node.js, which includes the npm (Node Package Manager) that you'll use to install TypeScript. You can download Node.js from nodejs.org.
2. **Install TypeScript via npm**
   Once Node.js is installed, you can use npm to install TypeScript globally. Open your terminal and run:

   ```bash
   npm install -g typescript
   ```

   This will make the TypeScript compiler (tsc) available globally on your machine.

3. **Verify the installation**
   After installation, you can verify that TypeScript is installed correctly by running:

   ```bash
   tsc --version
   ```

This command should return the version of TypeScript that is installed.

1.3 Setting Up Your First `tsconfig.json`

TypeScript uses a configuration file called `tsconfig.json` to control the behavior of the compiler. This file specifies things like where your source files are located, what types of files to include or exclude, and how the output should be structured.

Creating the `tsconfig.json` File

1. **Create a Project Directory**
   Start by creating a directory for your TypeScript project. For example:

   bash

   ```bash
   mkdir my-typescript-project
   cd my-typescript-project
   ```

2. **Initialize a TypeScript Project**
   Inside your project directory, initialize a `tsconfig.json` file by running:

   bash

   ```bash
   tsc --init
   ```

   This will create a `tsconfig.json` file with default settings.

3. **Understanding `tsconfig.json`**
   Here's a sample `tsconfig.json`:

   json

   ```json
   {
     "compilerOptions": {
       "target": "es5",
   ```

```
    "lib": ["dom", "es2015"],
    "outDir": "./dist",
    "rootDir": "./src",
    "strict": true
  },
  "include": ["src/**/*"],
  "exclude": ["node_modules"]
}
```

- o **compilerOptions**: Defines how the TypeScript
  compiler behaves. Here, we specify that our target
  JavaScript version is ES5, include support for
  ES2015 features, and enable strict type-checking.
- o **include**: Specifies the files that the compiler will
  include for compilation. The wildcard `src/**/*` tells
  the compiler to look in the `src` directory and all its
  subdirectories.
- o **exclude**: Excludes the `node_modules` directory
  from compilation (which is the default).
4. **Customizing the Configuration**
   You can adjust settings in `tsconfig.json` based on your
   project's needs. For example, setting `"noImplicitAny":
   true` will raise an error whenever TypeScript cannot infer
   the type of a variable (default behavior is to assume `any`
   type, which defeats the purpose of using TypeScript).

1.4 Basic Types: string, number, boolean, arrays, tuples, and type inference

One of the key features of TypeScript is its support for **static
typing**. Types in TypeScript help ensure that the values assigned
to variables are the expected type.

1.4.1 Primitive Types

TypeScript supports all the primitive types you might be familiar
with from JavaScript, with added type-checking:

- **string**: Represents text values.

```typescript
let name: string = "Alice";
```

- **number**: Represents numerical values (both integers and floats).

```typescript
let age: number = 25;
```

- **boolean**: Represents true or false values.

```typescript
let isActive: boolean = true;
```

1.4.2 Arrays

In TypeScript, you can specify the type of elements in an array:

```typescript
let numbers: number[] = [1, 2, 3];
let names: string[] = ["Alice", "Bob"];
```

Alternatively, you can use **tuple types**, which allow you to store multiple values of different types in a fixed order:

```typescript
let person: [string, number] = ["Alice", 25];
```

1.4.3 Type Inference

One of TypeScript's great features is **type inference**. TypeScript can automatically infer the type of a variable based on its value, even if you don't explicitly define the type.

For example:

```typescript
let greeting = "Hello, world!";  // TypeScript infers
that 'greeting' is of type string
```

While TypeScript does a great job of inferring types, it's always a good practice to be explicit about types for better clarity and to avoid errors.

1.5 Hands-on: Converting a Small JavaScript Snippet to TypeScript

Let's take a simple JavaScript function and convert it into TypeScript. Here's the original JavaScript code:

```javascript
function sum(a, b) {
    return a + b;
}
```

Now, let's convert this into TypeScript:

```typescript
function sum(a: number, b: number): number {
    return a + b;
}
```

<u>Explanation:</u>

- **Type Annotations**: We added : `number` to specify that both `a` and `b` are numbers, and the return value is also a number.
- **Type Checking**: Now, if you try to pass something other than a number, TypeScript will raise an error:

  ```typescript
  ```

```
sum(2, "hello");  // Error: Argument of type
'string' is not assignable to parameter of type
'number'.
```

1.6 Compilation Process

TypeScript needs to be **compiled** into JavaScript before it can run. You can do this manually by running the `tsc` command:

```bash
tsc sum.ts
```

This will generate a `sum.js` file with the compiled JavaScript. You can then run this JavaScript file in your browser or Node.js environment.

1.7 Inspecting the Output

After you compile your TypeScript code into JavaScript, the resulting JavaScript will look something like this:

```javascript
function sum(a, b) {
    return a + b;
}
```

Notice that TypeScript types are stripped out in the compiled JavaScript code, since JavaScript doesn't have a type system. However, TypeScript still adds value by catching errors during the development process, and the resulting JavaScript is **much safer** due to the stricter checks applied.

Chapter 2: Defining Interfaces and Type Aliases

2.1 Distinguishing Interface vs Type

In TypeScript, **interfaces** and **type aliases** are both used to describe the shape of data, but there are subtle differences in how they work and when to use them.

```
type Point = {
  x: number;
  y: number;
};
```

```
interface Point
  x: number;
  y: number
}
```

What is an Interface?

An **interface** is a structure used to define the shape of an object or function in a type-safe manner. It ensures that an object adheres to a particular structure, including its properties and methods.

typescript

```typescript
interface Person {
  name: string;
  age: number;
  greet(): void;
}

const person: Person = {
  name: "Alice",
  age: 30,
  greet() {
    console.log(`Hello, my name is ${this.name}.`);
  },
};
```

In the example above:

- The `Person` interface defines an object with a `name` property (of type `string`), an `age` property (of type `number`), and a `greet` method.
- The `person` object implements the interface, ensuring that it has all the required properties and methods.

Interfaces are **open-ended**, meaning you can extend them and add more properties or methods later. This makes them extremely flexible and reusable.

What is a Type Alias?

A **type alias** allows you to create a name for a specific type. You can use it to define object shapes, but type aliases are more versatile. They can represent not only objects but also primitive types, unions, intersections, and more.

```typescript
type Person = {
  name: string;
  age: number;
  greet(): void;
};

const person: Person = {
  name: "Bob",
  age: 25,
  greet() {
    console.log(`Hi, I'm ${this.name}`);
  },
};
```

While `type` and `interface` can both be used to describe object shapes, **type aliases** can also define **unions**, **intersections**, and even **primitive types**, whereas **interfaces** are more limited in that regard.

Key Differences

- **Extending and Merging**: Interfaces can be extended, while type aliases cannot be extended in the same way. However, type aliases can compose complex types using union and intersection types.
- **Declaration Merging**: Interfaces can have multiple declarations that get merged into a single interface. This is not possible with type aliases.

```typescript
interface Person {
  name: string;
}

interface Person {
```

```
  age: number;
}

const person: Person = {
  name: "Charlie",
  age: 28,
}; // This works due to declaration merging
```

2.2 Optional and Readonly Properties, Index Signatures

In TypeScript, interfaces and type aliases allow you to define properties with different behaviors. These include optional properties, readonly properties, and index signatures.

Optional Properties

Sometimes, not all properties of an object are required. TypeScript allows you to mark properties as **optional** using the ? operator.

```typescript
interface Person {
  name: string;
  age?: number; // age is optional
}

const person1: Person = { name: "Alice" }; // Valid
const person2: Person = { name: "Bob", age: 25 }; //
Valid
```

In the example above:

- The age property is optional, so we can create a Person object without providing an age.

Readonly Properties

If you want a property to be **immutable** (i.e., its value cannot be changed after initialization), you can use the `readonly` modifier.

typescript

```
interface Person {
  readonly name: string;
  age: number;
}

const person: Person = { name: "Charlie", age: 30 };
person.name = "Dave"; // Error: Cannot assign to
'name' because it is a read-only property
```

Here:

- The `name` property is marked as `readonly`, meaning it cannot be reassigned after the `Person` object is created.

Index Signatures

If you need to define an object with an unknown number of properties, you can use **index signatures**. These allow you to define the types of both keys and values dynamically.

typescript

```
interface Dictionary {
  [key: string]: string;
}

const dictionary: Dictionary = {
  "hello": "greeting",
  "world": "planet",
};
```

In this example:

- The index signature `[key: string]: string` means that the object can have any number of properties, as long as the keys are strings and the values are strings.

2.3 Union, Intersection, and Literal Types

TypeScript gives you the power to compose types using **unions**, **intersections**, and **literal types**. These features allow you to express complex data structures and ensure that the data adheres to the expected shape.

Union Types

A **union type** allows a variable to hold one of several types. You define a union by separating types with a pipe (|).

```typescript
type Status = "active" | "inactive" | "pending";

interface User {
  name: string;
  status: Status;
}

const user1: User = { name: "Alice", status: "active" }; // Valid
const user2: User = { name: "Bob", status: "inactive" }; // Valid
const user3: User = { name: "Charlie", status: "deleted" }; // Error: 'deleted' is not assignable to type 'Status'
```

Here:

- The `status` property can only be one of the specified literal values: `"active"`, `"inactive"`, or `"pending"`.
- Using union types ensures that only valid strings are assigned to the `status` property.

Intersection Types

An **intersection type** combines multiple types into one. The resulting type will include the properties of all the intersected types.

```typescript
typescript

interface Person {
  name: string;
}

interface Worker {
  job: string;
}

type Employee = Person & Worker;

const employee: Employee = { name: "Alice", job: "Engineer" };
```

In the example above:

- The `Employee` type is an intersection of `Person` and `Worker`, meaning that it must have both a `name` and a `job` property.

Literal Types

A **literal type** allows you to specify an exact value for a variable. Literal types ensure that only specific, predefined values can be assigned to a variable.

```typescript
typescript

type Direction = "up" | "down" | "left" | "right";

let move: Direction;
move = "up"; // Valid
move = "forward"; // Error: 'forward' is not
assignable to type 'Direction'
```

2.4 Hands-On: Building a Type-Safe Configuration Loader

In this section, we'll create a practical example to showcase how TypeScript's **type system** can help you build a **type-safe configuration loader**. This example will ensure that configuration data (often found in JSON files) adheres to a specific shape, and TypeScript will help us catch errors early.

Step 1: Defining the Configuration Shape

First, we define the shape of our configuration object using an interface:

```typescript
interface Config {
  apiUrl: string;
  apiKey: string;
  timeout: number;
}

const defaultConfig: Config = {
  apiUrl: "https://api.example.com",
  apiKey: "my-api-key",
  timeout: 5000,
};
```

Here:

- The `Config` interface defines the structure of the configuration object, with `apiUrl` and `apiKey` as strings and `timeout` as a number.

Step 2: Loading and Validating Configuration Data

Next, we build a function that loads configuration data from a JSON file and validates it against the `Config` interface. For simplicity, we will use `JSON.parse()` in this example.

```typescript
import * as fs from "fs";

function loadConfig(filePath: string): Config {
  const data = fs.readFileSync(filePath, "utf-8");
  const config = JSON.parse(data);

  // Validation to ensure the correct types
  if (typeof config.apiUrl !== "string") {
    throw new Error("Invalid apiUrl");
  }
  if (typeof config.apiKey !== "string") {
    throw new Error("Invalid apiKey");
  }
  if (typeof config.timeout !== "number") {
    throw new Error("Invalid timeout");
  }

  return config;
}
```

Step 3: Using the Configuration

Now we use the loader function to safely load and use our configuration data:

```typescript
try {
  const config = loadConfig("config.json");
  console.log(`API URL: ${config.apiUrl}`);
  console.log(`API Key: ${config.apiKey}`);
  console.log(`Timeout: ${config.timeout}`);
} catch (error) {
  console.error("Failed to load configuration:",
error);
}
```

Explanation

In this example:

- We define the expected structure of our configuration with the `Config` interface.
- The `loadConfig` function reads the JSON file, parses it, and performs manual type checks to ensure that the data matches the expected shape.
- If the data doesn't match, an error is thrown, and TypeScript ensures that our types are validated at compile time, giving us extra confidence that we're using the correct structure.

Conclusion

This chapter provided an in-depth look at defining **interfaces** and **type aliases** in TypeScript. We explored the core differences between the two, how to use them to define shapes of data, and various advanced techniques such as **optional properties**, **readonly properties**, **index signatures**, and **union/intersection types**.

With the hands-on configuration loader project, you learned how to ensure that the data you work with adheres to a specific structure, which is a critical aspect of building type-safe, robust applications.

Chapter 3: Mastering Generics

3.1 Introduction to Generics

Generics in TypeScript allow you to write reusable, flexible, and type-safe code that can work with various data types. Rather than hard-coding the type of a variable, function, or class, generics let you define types as placeholders that can be specified later.

Think of generics as **"templates"** for types. They allow functions and classes to work with any data type, yet still maintain the power of type-checking, ensuring the safety and consistency of your code.

For example, rather than writing a function that only works with strings or only works with numbers, you can create a function that works with any type. This makes your code highly reusable and eliminates the need to duplicate logic for different types.

Let's dive deeper into the main topics related to generics and explore them step by step.

3.2 Generic Functions

3.2.1 Basic Syntax

A **generic function** allows you to define a function that can accept arguments of different types and return values of different types, while still maintaining the safety that TypeScript provides.

Here's a simple example of a generic function:

```typescript
function identity<T>(value: T): T {
  return value;
```

```
}
```

- **T** is the placeholder for a type that will be specified when the function is called.
- The function `identity` takes a parameter `value` of type `T` and returns a value of the same type `T`.

3.2.2 Calling Generic Functions

When you call the `identity` function, TypeScript automatically infers the type, but you can also explicitly specify the type.

```typescript
let num = identity(123);   // TypeScript infers 'T' as
number
let str = identity("hello");   // TypeScript infers
'T' as string

// Explicit type
let bool = identity<boolean>(true);   // You can
specify 'boolean' as the type
```

3.2.3 Benefits of Generic Functions

Generic functions allow us to:

- **Avoid duplication**: You don't need to write multiple versions of the same function for different types.
- **Type safety**: Even though the function is flexible, TypeScript will still catch errors at compile time if you try to pass the wrong type.

3.3 Generic Classes

Just like functions, **generic classes** allow you to define classes that can work with any type.

3.3.1 Defining a Generic Class

Here's an example of a generic class that holds a value of a specified type:

typescript

```
class Box<T> {
  private value: T;

  constructor(value: T) {
    this.value = value;
  }

  getValue(): T {
    return this.value;
  }
}
```

- The class `Box` uses a generic type `T` for the `value` property, meaning that `value` can be of any type.
- The `getValue` method returns the value of the same type `T`.

3.3.2 Using Generic Classes

Now you can create instances of `Box` with any type you choose:

typescript

```
const numBox = new Box<number>(123);
console.log(numBox.getValue()); // Output: 123

const strBox = new Box<string>("hello");
console.log(strBox.getValue()); // Output: hello
```

In this example, `numBox` holds a `number`, and `strBox` holds a `string`, and TypeScript ensures type safety at every step.

3.4 Generic Constraints

Sometimes you may want to limit the types that can be used with a generic function or class. This is where **constraints** come into play.

3.4.1 Adding Constraints to Generics

You can add a constraint to a generic by using the `extends` keyword. For example, let's say you only want to allow types that have a `length` property (such as `string` or `array`).

typescript

```typescript
function logLength<T extends { length: number
}>(item: T): void {
  console.log(item.length);
}
```

In this case:

- `T extends { length: number }` means that `T` must be a type that has a `length` property of type `number`.

3.4.2 Using Constraints

Now, you can only pass objects or arrays with a `length` property to the `logLength` function:

typescript

```typescript
logLength("Hello, World!");  // Valid
logLength([1, 2, 3]);  // Valid
logLength(123);  // Error: Argument of type 'number'
is not assignable to parameter of type 'length:
number'
```

This constraint ensures that the function is only used with types that support the `length` property.

3.5 Utility Types: Partial, Pick, Record, and More

TypeScript comes with a set of built-in **utility types** that can be used to modify or create new types from existing ones. These utility types can be highly valuable when working with complex data structures.

3.5.1 Partial

The `Partial` utility type makes all properties of a given type optional.

```typescript
interface User {
  name: string;
  age: number;
}

const updateUser = (user: Partial<User>) => {
  console.log(user);
};

updateUser({ name: "Alice" }); // Valid, age is optional
```

- `Partial<User>` means that all properties in the `User` interface are optional. This is useful when you're working with partial data, such as when updating an object.

3.5.2 Pick

The `Pick` utility type allows you to create a new type by picking specific properties from an existing type.

```typescript
interface User {
```

```
  name: string;
  age: number;
  email: string;
}

type UserProfile = Pick<User, "name" | "email">;
const profile: UserProfile = { name: "Bob", email:
"bob@example.com" };
```

- Pick<User, "name" | "email"> creates a new type with only the name and email properties from the User interface.

3.5.3 Record

The Record utility type creates a type with a specific set of keys and values.

```typescript

type UserPermissions = Record<string, boolean>;

const permissions: UserPermissions = {
  "view": true,
  "edit": false,
  "delete": true,
};
```

- Record<string, boolean> means that the keys of permissions are of type string, and the values are of type boolean.

3.5.4 Other Utility Types

TypeScript also provides other utility types like Readonly, Exclude, and Extract. Each has its specific use case, but the core idea is that these utilities allow you to manipulate and transform types in powerful ways.

3.6 Custom Mapped Types

Mapped types allow you to create new types by transforming the properties of an existing type.

3.6.1 Basic Mapped Types

For example, you can create a new type where all properties of an existing type are **readonly**:

```typescript
typescript

type ReadonlyUser = { readonly [K in keyof User]:
User[K] };
```

Here:

- `ReadonlyUser` is a new type where all properties of `User` are marked as `readonly`.

3.6.2 Making Properties Optional

You can also create a mapped type that makes all properties optional:

```typescript
typescript

type OptionalUser = { [K in keyof User]?: User[K] };
```

- `OptionalUser` creates a new type where all properties from `User` are optional.

3.7 Conditional Types

Conditional types in TypeScript allow you to define a type based on a **condition**. You can think of them as type-level **if-else** statements.

3.7.1 Basic Syntax

Here's a basic example:

```typescript
type IsString<T> = T extends string ? "Yes" : "No";
```

- If `T` is a `string`, `IsString<T>` will evaluate to `"Yes"`, otherwise it will evaluate to `"No"`.

3.7.2 Using Conditional Types

Let's use a conditional type to create a type that checks whether a type is a `string` or not:

```typescript
type IsString<T> = T extends string ? "Yes" : "No";

type Test1 = IsString<string>;  // "Yes"
type Test2 = IsString<number>;  // "No"
```

This way, you can create types that depend on other types, adding an extra layer of flexibility to your TypeScript code.

3.8 Hands-On Project: Creating a Reusable Generic Data Service

Now, let's put everything we've learned into action by creating a **reusable generic data service** that fetches and caches API responses. This service will be type-safe, and TypeScript will ensure that the data returned from the API matches the expected shape.

3.8.1 Defining the Data Service

We'll start by defining a class `DataService` that is generic, meaning it can work with any type of data returned from an API.

typescript

```
class DataService<T> {
  private cache: Map<string, T> = new Map();

  async fetchData(url: string): Promise<T> {
    if (this.cache.has(url)) {
      console.log("Returning cached data...");
      return this.cache.get(url)!;
    }

    const response = await fetch(url);
    const data: T = await response.json();
    this.cache.set(url, data);
    return data;
  }
}
```

Here:

- The `DataService` class uses a generic type `T`, so it can work with any type of data.
- The `fetchData` method retrieves data from an API and caches it for future use.

3.8.2 Using the Data Service

Now, let's use the `DataService` class to fetch data from an API and ensure type safety:

```typescript
interface User {
  id: number;
  name: string;
}

const userService = new DataService<User>();

userService.fetchData("https://api.example.com/users/
1").then((user) => {
  console.log(user.name); // TypeScript knows `user`
has a `name` property.
});
```

In this example:

- We define an interface `User` to specify the shape of the data returned from the API.
- We create an instance of `DataService` with `User` as the generic type.
- TypeScript ensures that the `user` object returned by `fetchData` has the expected properties.

Conclusion

In this chapter, we've covered the essentials of **generics** in TypeScript, including **generic functions**, **generic classes**, **constraints**, **utility types**, **custom mapped types**, and **conditional types**. By the end of this chapter, you should have a solid understanding of how to use generics to write flexible, reusable, and type-safe code.

In the hands-on project, we built a **generic data service** to fetch and cache API responses, reinforcing how generics work in real-world applications.

Chapter 4: Object-Oriented Patterns in TypeScript

4.1 Introduction to Object-Oriented Programming (OOP)

Object-Oriented Programming (OOP) is a programming paradigm based on the concept of "objects." These objects can contain both **data** (attributes or properties) and **methods** (functions or behaviors). OOP allows for better organization, scalability, and maintainability of code, especially in large projects.

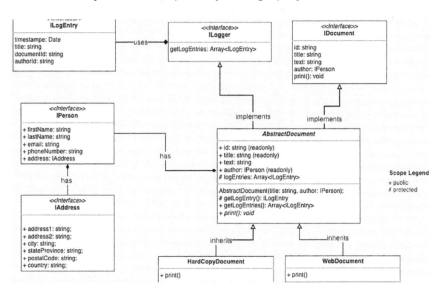

TypeScript is a superset of JavaScript, which means it supports all of JavaScript's features, including those that align with OOP principles. However, TypeScript also introduces **static typing** and other advanced features like **interfaces** and **generics**, making it an ideal choice for building scalable object-oriented applications.

In this chapter, we will walk through the key OOP patterns and principles in TypeScript, focusing on **classes**, **inheritance**, **abstract classes**, **implementing interfaces**, **access modifiers**, **parameter properties**, **mixins**, and **decorators**.

4.2 Classes in TypeScript

A **class** in TypeScript is a blueprint for creating objects with predefined properties and methods. Classes provide a way to bundle data (properties) and functionality (methods) together.

4.2.1 Defining a Class

Here's an example of how to define a simple class in TypeScript:

```typescript
class Animal {
  name: string;
  constructor(name: string) {
    this.name = name;
  }

  speak() {
    console.log(`${this.name} makes a sound.`);
  }
}

const dog = new Animal("Dog");
dog.speak(); // Output: Dog makes a sound.
```

- **Properties**: In the example above, `name` is a property of the `Animal` class.
- **Constructor**: The `constructor` is a special method used to initialize objects when they are created.
- **Method**: The `speak()` method prints a message when called.

4.2.2 Instantiating Classes

To create an object from a class, you use the `new` keyword:

typescript

```typescript
const cat = new Animal("Cat");
cat.speak(); // Output: Cat makes a sound.
```

Each instance of the `Animal` class has its own `name` property, allowing you to create different animals with different names.

4.3 Inheritance in TypeScript

One of the most important features of OOP is **inheritance**. Inheritance allows a class (the **child** or **subclass**) to inherit properties and methods from another class (the **parent** or **superclass**). This promotes **code reuse** and the creation of more specialized classes.

4.3.1 Inheriting from a Class

You can extend a class in TypeScript using the `extends` keyword. Here's how you can create a `Dog` class that inherits from the `Animal` class:

typescript

```typescript
class Dog extends Animal {
  breed: string;

  constructor(name: string, breed: string) {
    super(name); // Call the parent class constructor
    this.breed = breed;
  }

  speak() {
    console.log(`${this.name} barks.`);
```

```
  }
}

const dog = new Dog("Buddy", "Golden Retriever");
dog.speak(); // Output: Buddy barks.
```

In this example:

- The `Dog` class extends the `Animal` class, so it inherits the `name` property and `speak()` method.
- The `Dog` class also adds a new property `breed` and overrides the `speak()` method to provide a custom implementation.

4.3.2 Using the `super` Keyword

The `super` keyword is used to call the constructor of the parent class and initialize inherited properties. Without `super()`, the child class cannot access the parent class's constructor.

4.4 Abstract Classes and the `abstract` Keyword

An **abstract class** is a class that cannot be instantiated on its own but serves as a base class for other classes. It allows you to define common properties and methods that can be inherited by subclasses while also defining **abstract methods** that must be implemented by subclasses.

4.4.1 Defining an Abstract Class

```typescript
abstract class Animal {
  name: string;

  constructor(name: string) {
    this.name = name;
  }
```

```
  abstract speak(): void; // Abstract method
}

class Dog extends Animal {
  speak() {
    console.log(`${this.name} barks.`);
  }
}

const dog = new Dog("Buddy");
dog.speak(); // Output: Buddy barks.
```

In this example:

- The `Animal` class is abstract and has an abstract method `speak()`.
- The `Dog` class extends `Animal` and implements the `speak()` method.

4.4.2 When to Use Abstract Classes

Use abstract classes when you want to provide a common structure or shared behavior for multiple subclasses, but prevent direct instantiation of the base class itself.

4.5 Implementing Interfaces in TypeScript

In TypeScript, **interfaces** define a contract for classes to follow. A class that implements an interface is required to implement all the methods and properties defined by the interface.

4.5.1 Defining an Interface

```
typescript

interface Speaker {
  speak(): void;
}
```

```
class Dog implements Speaker {
  speak() {
    console.log("Woof!");
  }
}

class Cat implements Speaker {
  speak() {
    console.log("Meow!");
  }
}

const dog = new Dog();
dog.speak(); // Output: Woof!

const cat = new Cat();
cat.speak(); // Output: Meow!
```

In this example:

- The `Speaker` interface defines the `speak()` method.
- Both `Dog` and `Cat` implement the `Speaker` interface and must provide their own implementation of `speak()`.

4.5.2 Why Use Interfaces?

Interfaces allow for a more flexible and decoupled design. By defining a contract, interfaces ensure that any class that implements the interface will adhere to the expected structure, making the code more predictable and easier to maintain.

4.6 Access Modifiers and Parameter Properties

Access modifiers in TypeScript control the visibility of class properties and methods. They can be set to **public**, **private**, or **protected**.

4.6.1 Public, Private, and Protected

- **Public** (default): The property or method is accessible from anywhere.
- **Private**: The property or method can only be accessed within the class.
- **Protected**: The property or method can be accessed within the class and by subclasses.

```typescript
class Animal {
  public name: string;
  private age: number;
  protected sound: string;

  constructor(name: string, age: number, sound: string) {
    this.name = name;
    this.age = age;
    this.sound = sound;
  }
}

const animal = new Animal("Lion", 5, "Roar");
console.log(animal.name); // Accessible
// console.log(animal.age); // Error: Property 'age' is private
// console.log(animal.sound); // Error: Property 'sound' is protected
```

4.6.2 Parameter Properties

TypeScript allows you to define **parameter properties** directly in the constructor, reducing the need for additional property declarations.

```typescript
class Animal {
  constructor(public name: string, private age: number) {}
```

```
}

const dog = new Animal("Buddy", 3);
console.log(dog.name); // Accessible
// console.log(dog.age); // Error: Property 'age' is
private
```

In this example:

- The `name` property is automatically assigned from the constructor and is public.
- The `age` property is private, so it can only be accessed within the class.

4.7 Mixins and Decorators Overview

4.7.1 Mixins

A **mixin** is a way to extend functionality in TypeScript. Mixins allow you to add properties and methods from one class into another without using inheritance.

```typescript
class CanFly {
  fly() {
    console.log("Flying!");
  }
}

class CanSwim {
  swim() {
    console.log("Swimming!");
  }
}

class Duck implements CanFly, CanSwim {
  constructor() {}
}
```

```
applyMixins(Duck, [CanFly, CanSwim]);

const duck = new Duck();
duck.fly(); // Output: Flying!
duck.swim(); // Output: Swimming!

function applyMixins(derivedCtor: any, baseCtors:
any[]) {
  baseCtors.forEach(baseCtor => {

Object.getOwnPropertyNames(baseCtor.prototype).forEac
h(name => {
      derivedCtor.prototype[name] =
baseCtor.prototype[name];
    });
  });
}
```

In this example:

- We define two mixin classes `CanFly` and `CanSwim` that add specific functionalities (methods).
- The `Duck` class implements both mixins using `applyMixins`, giving it both the ability to fly and swim.

4.7.2 Decorators

Decorators in TypeScript are special functions that can be attached to classes, methods, or properties to modify their behavior. They are often used in frameworks like Angular.

```typescript
function Log(target: any, propertyKey: string) {
  console.log(`Property ${propertyKey} has been
accessed.`);
}

class Animal {
  @Log
  name: string;
```

```
  constructor(name: string) {
    this.name = name;
  }
}

const animal = new Animal("Lion");
console.log(animal.name); // Output: Property name
has been accessed.
```

In this example:

- The @Log decorator is applied to the name property.
- Every time name is accessed, the decorator logs a message.

4.8 Hands-On Project: Designing a Plugin Framework

In this section, we will create a **plugin framework** where each plugin implements a standard interface. This project will incorporate the concepts of classes, interfaces, inheritance, and decorators, helping solidify your understanding of OOP in TypeScript.

4.8.1 Defining the Plugin Interface

We start by defining the interface that all plugins must implement:

```
typescript

interface Plugin {
  name: string;
  run(): void;
}
```

4.8.2 Creating Plugins

Next, we'll create two plugins that implement the `Plugin` interface:

typescript

```typescript
class LoggerPlugin implements Plugin {
  name = "Logger";

  run() {
    console.log("Running Logger Plugin...");
  }
}

class AnalyticsPlugin implements Plugin {
  name = "Analytics";

  run() {
    console.log("Running Analytics Plugin...");
  }
}
```

4.8.3 Plugin Manager

Finally, we'll create a `PluginManager` class to manage and execute plugins:

typescript

```typescript
class PluginManager {
  private plugins: Plugin[] = [];

  addPlugin(plugin: Plugin) {
    this.plugins.push(plugin);
  }

  runAll() {
    this.plugins.forEach(plugin => plugin.run());
  }
}

const manager = new PluginManager();
manager.addPlugin(new LoggerPlugin());
```

```
manager.addPlugin(new AnalyticsPlugin());
manager.runAll();
```

In this example:

- The `PluginManager` class stores a collection of plugins
  and provides a method to run all plugins.

Conclusion

In this chapter, we've covered core **object-oriented
programming (OOP) patterns** in TypeScript, including **classes**,
inheritance, **abstract classes**, **interfaces**, **access modifiers**,
parameter properties, **mixins**, and **decorators**. With these
concepts, you can design clean, reusable, and maintainable code.

The **hands-on plugin framework** project demonstrated how to
apply these OOP principles in a real-world scenario. By designing
a framework where plugins implement a standard interface, we
showed how TypeScript's OOP features can be used to build
flexible and scalable applications.

Chapter 5: Managing Asynchronous Code

5.1 Introduction to Asynchronous Programming

Asynchronous programming allows a program to perform tasks **concurrently** without blocking the main execution thread. This is particularly useful in web development where tasks like **fetching data from APIs**, **reading files**, or **waiting for user input** can take time, and you don't want the entire application to freeze while waiting for these operations to complete.

In JavaScript (and TypeScript), **asynchronous operations** are managed through **callbacks**, **Promises**, and more recently, **async/await**. TypeScript, as a superset of JavaScript, provides these same mechanisms, but with the added benefit of **static typing**, making it easier to catch errors at compile-time.

Let's break down the main ways asynchronous code is handled and then dive into advanced patterns for error handling, and retry strategies, and explore RxJS for more complex scenarios.

5.2 Promises vs async/await

5.2.1 Understanding Promises

A **Promise** is an object that represents a value which may be available now, or in the future, or never. It is a way to handle asynchronous operations and manage their eventual completion or failure.

A Promise can be in one of the following states:

- **Pending**: The operation is still in progress.
- **Fulfilled**: The operation completed successfully.
- **Rejected**: The operation failed.

Here's a simple example of a Promise:

typescript

```
const fetchData = new Promise<string>((resolve,
reject) => {
  setTimeout(() => {
    const data = "Hello, world!";
    resolve(data); // Fulfills the promise with
"Hello, world!"
  }, 1000);
});

fetchData.then(data => console.log(data));  //
Output: Hello, world!
```

In the above example:

- `resolve(data)` fulfills the promise with a value, and `then` is used to handle the fulfillment.
- If something goes wrong during the operation, `reject()` can be called to handle errors.

5.2.2 Using Promises for Asynchronous Operations

Promises can also be chained to manage sequences of asynchronous operations. Here's an example:

typescript

```
function fetchDataFromAPI(): Promise<string> {
  return new Promise((resolve, reject) => {
    setTimeout(() => {
      const data = "API response";
      resolve(data);
    }, 2000);
  });
```

```
}

fetchDataFromAPI()
   .then(data => {
      console.log(data); // Output: API response
      return "Next data";
   })
   .then(nextData => console.log(nextData));   //
Output: Next data
```

In this example:

- Each `then()` returns a new Promise, allowing for **chaining** of multiple asynchronous actions.

5.2.3 Introducing async/await

`async/await` is a syntactic sugar built on top of Promises. It makes asynchronous code look and behave more like **synchronous code**, allowing you to write asynchronous logic without the need for chaining `.then()` or `.catch()` methods.

An `async` function automatically returns a **Promise**, and the `await` keyword pauses the function's execution until the Promise is resolved or rejected.

```typescript
async function fetchData(): Promise<string> {
   const data = await fetchDataFromAPI(); // wait
until fetchDataFromAPI() resolves
   console.log(data); // Output: API response
   return data;
}
```

Here:

- The `await` keyword waits for the `fetchDataFromAPI()` Promise to resolve before continuing with the execution.

- This makes it easier to read and understand asynchronous code because it doesn't have nested callbacks or chained `.then()` statements.

5.2.4 Comparison: Promises vs async/await

Aspect	Promises	async/await
Syntax	`.then()`, `.catch()` for chaining	Synchronous-looking code
Error handling	`.catch()` method for error handling	`try/catch` blocks
Readability	Can become hard to read with chaining	More natural, easier to read
Compatibility	Supported in all modern browsers	Supported in ES2017+ (modern browsers)

5.2.5 Error Handling with Promises and async/await

Handling errors in asynchronous code is crucial. Both Promises and async/await allow for error handling, but the syntax differs.

- **With Promises**, you handle errors using `.catch()`:

typescript

```typescript
fetchDataFromAPI()
  .then(data => console.log(data))
  .catch(error => console.error("Error:", error));
```

- **With async/await**, you use `try/catch` blocks:

typescript

```typescript
async function fetchData() {
  try {
    const data = await fetchDataFromAPI();
    console.log(data);
  } catch (error) {
    console.error("Error:", error);
  }
}
```

Using `try/catch` with async/await makes error handling in asynchronous code more intuitive, as it resembles how errors are handled in synchronous code.

5.3 Error Handling Patterns and Custom Error Types

Handling errors properly in asynchronous code is critical for building reliable and user-friendly applications. TypeScript provides several techniques for managing errors, including custom error types and strategies for retrying operations.

5.3.1 Default Error Handling

In both `Promises` and `async/await`, errors are typically caught via the `catch()` method or `try/catch` block. However, creating custom error types can provide more meaningful information when things go wrong.

5.3.2 Creating Custom Error Types

In TypeScript, you can create custom error classes by extending the built-in `Error` class:

```typescript
class ApiError extends Error {
  statusCode: number;

  constructor(message: string, statusCode: number) {
    super(message);  // Call parent class constructor
with message
    this.name = "ApiError";
    this.statusCode = statusCode;
  }
}
```

```
function throwError() {
  throw new ApiError("API request failed", 500);
}

try {
  throwError();
} catch (error) {
  if (error instanceof ApiError) {
    console.error(`Error: ${error.message}, Status:
${error.statusCode}`);
  }
}
```

In this example:

- `ApiError` extends the built-in `Error` class, adding a
  `statusCode` property.
- Using `instanceof`, you can check the error type and
  handle it appropriately.

5.3.3 Exponential Backoff for Retries

Exponential backoff is a strategy to handle retries in the event of
an error. The idea is to wait progressively longer between retries
to avoid overwhelming the system or API.

```typescript
async function fetchDataWithRetry(url: string,
retries: number = 3, delay: number = 1000):
Promise<any> {
  for (let attempt = 1; attempt <= retries;
attempt++) {
    try {
      const response = await fetch(url);
      if (!response.ok) {
        throw new Error("Failed to fetch");
      }
      return await response.json();
    } catch (error) {
      if (attempt === retries) {
```

```
      throw new Error("Max retries reached");
    }
    console.log(`Retrying in ${delay}ms...`);
    await new Promise(resolve =>
setTimeout(resolve, delay));
    delay *= 2;   // Exponential backoff
   }
  }
}

fetchDataWithRetry("https://api.example.com/data")
  .then(data => console.log(data))
  .catch(error => console.error(error));
```

In this function:

- The code retries the operation `retries` times.
- After each failed attempt, the `delay` is doubled,
  implementing exponential backoff.

5.4 Intro to RxJS and Observables

5.4.1 What is RxJS?

RxJS (Reactive Extensions for JavaScript) is a library for handling
asynchronous and event-based programming using **Observables**.
Observables are a powerful abstraction that allows you to manage
streams of data over time, enabling a more declarative approach
to handling asynchronous operations.

5.4.2 Working with Observables

An **Observable** is a data stream that can be subscribed to. Unlike
Promises, which resolve once, Observables can emit multiple
values over time.

Here's a simple example:

```typescript
import { Observable } from 'rxjs';

const observable = new Observable<number>(subscriber
=> {
  let count = 0;
  setInterval(() => {
    subscriber.next(count++);
    if (count === 5) {
      subscriber.complete();
    }
  }, 1000);
});

observable.subscribe({
  next: value => console.log(value),    // On each
emission
  complete: () => console.log('Complete') // When the
observable completes
});
```

In this example:

- An Observable emits numbers every second.
- The `subscribe()` method listens for emissions and reacts to them.

5.4.3 Operators in RxJS

RxJS provides a wide range of operators to manipulate Observables, such as `map`, `filter`, `mergeMap`, and `concatMap`.

```typescript
import { from } from 'rxjs';
import { map } from 'rxjs/operators';

const numbers = from([1, 2, 3, 4]);
numbers.pipe(map(x => x * 2)).subscribe(console.log);
// Output: 2, 4, 6, 8
```

In this example:

- The `map` operator is used to multiply each emitted value by 2.

5.5 Hands-On Project: Typed Data-Fetch Module with Exponential Backoff

Now, let's apply what we've learned by building a **typed data-fetch module** that retries failed requests using exponential backoff. This module will handle errors gracefully, provide meaningful messages, and retry on failure, which is a common pattern when working with APIs.

```typescript
type FetchOptions = {
  retries: number;
  delay: number;
};

async function fetchWithExponentialBackoff<T>(url:
string, options: FetchOptions): Promise<T> {
  let { retries, delay } = options;

  for (let attempt = 1; attempt <= retries;
attempt++) {
    try {
      const response = await fetch(url);
      if (!response.ok) {
        throw new Error("Network response was not
ok");
      }
      return await response.json();
    } catch (error) {
      if (attempt === retries) {
        throw new Error("Max retries reached");
      }
```

```
      console.log(`Attempt ${attempt} failed.
Retrying in ${delay}ms...`);
      await new Promise(resolve =>
setTimeout(resolve, delay));
      delay *= 2;   // Exponential backoff
    }
  }
}

// Usage
fetchWithExponentialBackoff("https://api.example.com/
data", { retries: 5, delay: 1000 })
  .then(data => console.log(data))
  .catch(error => console.error("Final error:",
error));
```

In this project:

- **Type safety** is maintained by using a generic type T, ensuring the correct type of data is fetched.
- **Exponential backoff** is implemented to delay retries progressively.
- **Error handling** is robust, using retries and logging for feedback.

Conclusion

In this chapter, we covered **managing asynchronous code** in TypeScript. From **Promises** and **async/await** to more advanced concepts like **error handling**, **exponential backoff**, and **RxJS**, we learned how to handle asynchronous operations efficiently and safely.

By building a **typed data-fetch module with retries** using exponential backoff, you now have a practical tool for managing asynchronous tasks in your own applications. Whether you're working with APIs or performing complex data operations, these patterns will help you write more robust, maintainable, and resilient code.

Chapter 6: Tooling, Linting, and Formatting

6.1 Introduction to Tooling in TypeScript Development

As your TypeScript projects grow, managing configuration, formatting, and linting becomes crucial for maintaining code quality and consistency. **Tooling** refers to the various utilities and configurations you use to enhance your development process, including:

- TypeScript's compiler (`tsc`)
- Code linting tools (e.g., **ESLint**)
- Code formatting tools (e.g., **Prettier**)
- Build automation (e.g., **Webpack**, **GitHub Actions**)

Using these tools properly can save you time and effort, improve team collaboration, and ensure that your code adheres to best practices. In this chapter, we'll explore the following key topics:

1. Configuring `tsconfig.json` for different targets.
2. Setting up **ESLint** with TypeScript rules and integrating **Prettier** for formatting.
3. Automating build and type checks directly within your editor.
4. Creating a **GitHub Actions** workflow to automate linting, testing, and building on each code push.

6.2 Crafting a Solid `tsconfig.json` for Different Targets

The `tsconfig.json` file is the backbone of any TypeScript project. It defines the TypeScript compiler's behavior, including which files are compiled, what language features to use, and where to output the compiled JavaScript code. A well-configured `tsconfig.json` file ensures consistent builds across different environments and targets.

6.2.1 Basic Structure of `tsconfig.json`

A typical `tsconfig.json` file looks like this:

json

```json
{
  "compilerOptions": {
    "target": "es5",
    "module": "commonjs",
    "strict": true,
    "esModuleInterop": true,
    "skipLibCheck": true,
    "forceConsistentCasingInFileNames": true,
    "outDir": "./dist",
    "rootDir": "./src"
  },
  "include": [
    "src/**/*.ts"
  ],
  "exclude": [
    "node_modules"
  ]
}
```

- **compilerOptions**: Defines the options for how TypeScript should compile your code.
    - **target**: Specifies the JavaScript version to target (e.g., es5, es6, esnext). The `target` option ensures that the TypeScript compiler generates

code compatible with the specified version of JavaScript.

- o **module**: Defines the module system (e.g., `commonjs`, `esnext`).
- o **strict**: Enforces stricter type checking, which helps catch potential errors earlier.
- o **outDir**: Specifies the directory where the compiled JavaScript files will be placed.
- o **rootDir**: Specifies the root directory of your TypeScript files.
- **include**: Specifies which files to include in the compilation (e.g., `src/**/*.ts` includes all TypeScript files in the `src` directory and its subdirectories).
- **exclude**: Specifies which files to exclude (e.g., `node_modules` is excluded by default).

6.2.2 Configuring for Different Targets

You may want your TypeScript project to work across different environments, such as browsers, Node.js, or hybrid applications. You can tailor your `tsconfig.json` to target multiple environments by customizing the compiler options.

For example, to support both **ES6** and **CommonJS** modules, you might set the `module` and `target` options differently:

json

```json
{
  "compilerOptions": {
    "target": "es6",  // ES6 for modern browsers and Node.js
    "module": "commonjs"  // CommonJS for Node.js compatibility
  }
}
```

If you're building a project for the **browser**, you might also use a module system like `esnext` or `system`, which is suited for modern JavaScript module bundlers like **Webpack** or **Rollup**.

For **Node.js** projects, you may choose `commonjs` for compatibility with the Node.js module system.

6.2.3 Advanced Configurations

1. **Path Aliases**: You can configure path aliases to simplify imports. This is especially useful in larger projects with deep folder structures.

json

```json
{
  "compilerOptions": {
    "baseUrl": "./src",
    "paths": {
      "@components/*": ["components/*"],
      "@utils/*": ["utils/*"]
    }
  }
}
```

- In this example, you can import files using `@components` or `@utils` as aliases instead of relative paths like `../../../utils`.

2. **Module Resolution**: You can configure how TypeScript resolves modules. This is useful when your code depends on a custom module resolution strategy or you are working with packages that use different formats.

json

```json
{
  "compilerOptions": {
    "moduleResolution": "node"
  }
```

}

6.3 Setting Up ESLint with TypeScript Rules and Prettier

ESLint is a powerful tool for identifying and fixing problems in your JavaScript and TypeScript code. It analyzes your code and enforces a set of rules for consistency, readability, and error prevention. **Prettier** is an opinionated code formatter that helps maintain consistent code formatting across your project.

6.3.1 Installing ESLint and Prettier

To get started, install ESLint and Prettier in your project:

bash

```
npm install --save-dev eslint @typescript-
eslint/parser @typescript-eslint/eslint-plugin
prettier eslint-config-prettier eslint-plugin-
prettier
```

- **eslint**: The core ESLint package.
- **@typescript-eslint/parser**: The parser that allows ESLint to parse TypeScript code.
- **@typescript-eslint/eslint-plugin**: The TypeScript-specific ESLint rules.
- **prettier**: The Prettier code formatter.
- **eslint-config-prettier**: Disables ESLint rules that conflict with Prettier.
- **eslint-plugin-prettier**: Integrates Prettier with ESLint.

6.3.2 Configuring ESLint for TypeScript

Create an `.eslintrc.json` file in the root of your project to configure ESLint:

json

```json
{
  "parser": "@typescript-eslint/parser",
  "extends": [
    "eslint:recommended",
    "plugin:@typescript-eslint/recommended",
    "plugin:prettier/recommended"
  ],
  "env": {
    "es2021": true,
    "node": true
  },
  "parserOptions": {
    "ecmaVersion": 12,
    "sourceType": "module"
  },
  "rules": {
    "@typescript-eslint/no-explicit-any": "warn",
    "prettier/prettier": "error"
  }
}
```

- **parser**: Uses `@typescript-eslint/parser` to parse TypeScript code.
- **extends**: Inherits configuration from popular ESLint, TypeScript, and Prettier presets.
- **parserOptions**: Specifies ECMAScript version and module type.
- **rules**: Defines custom rules, such as warning on the use of `any` type and making Prettier issues errors.

6.3.3 Configuring Prettier

Create a `.prettierrc` configuration file to specify Prettier's formatting rules:

json

```json
{
  "semi": true,
  "singleQuote": true,
```

```
  "trailingComma": "all",
  "tabWidth": 2
}
```

- **semi**: Adds semicolons at the end of statements.
- **singleQuote**: Uses single quotes for strings instead of double quotes.
- **trailingComma**: Includes trailing commas in multi-line lists for cleaner diffs.
- **tabWidth**: Sets the number of spaces per indentation level.

6.3.4 Running ESLint and Prettier

You can run ESLint and Prettier manually using the following commands:

bash

```bash
npx eslint . --fix    # Fixes ESLint errors automatically
npx prettier --write .   # Auto-formats the code using Prettier
```

To streamline the process, consider adding these commands to your `package.json`:

json

```json
"scripts": {
  "lint": "eslint . --fix",
  "format": "prettier --write ."
}
```

Now you can run `npm run lint` and `npm run format` to automatically lint and format your code.

6.4 Automating Builds and Type Checks in Your Editor

To speed up your development process and catch issues early, automating builds and type checks directly in your editor is a good practice. Most modern IDEs (like **VS Code**) support integration with TypeScript, ESLint, and Prettier.

6.4.1 Setting Up Type Checking in VS Code

To enable TypeScript type checking directly in **VS Code**, ensure that you have the **TypeScript** extension installed. You can then configure VS Code to perform **real-time type checking** by adding the following to your settings:

json

```json
{
  "typescript.validate.enable": true,
  "eslint.enable": true,
  "editor.formatOnSave": true
}
```

- **typescript.validate.enable**: Ensures VS Code checks TypeScript files for type errors.
- **eslint.enable**: Enables ESLint integration in VS Code.
- **editor.formatOnSave**: Automatically formats files with Prettier when you save them.

6.5 Hands-On: Configure a GitHub Actions Workflow

Automating your build, linting, and testing processes is essential for ensuring consistency across your development and CI/CD environments. Let's create a **GitHub Actions** workflow that automatically lints, tests, and builds your project whenever code is pushed to your repository.

6.5.1 Setting Up GitHub Actions

1. In your repository, create a `.github/workflows` directory.
2. Inside this directory, create a file named `ci.yml`:

```yaml
name: CI Workflow

on:
  push:
    branches:
      - main
  pull_request:
    branches:
      - main

jobs:
  lint:
    runs-on: ubuntu-latest
    steps:
      - name: Checkout code
        uses: actions/checkout@v2
      - name: Set up Node.js
        uses: actions/setup-node@v2
        with:
          node-version: '14'
      - name: Install dependencies
        run: npm install
      - name: Run ESLint
        run: npm run lint

  test:
    runs-on: ubuntu-latest
    steps:
      - name: Checkout code
        uses: actions/checkout@v2
      - name: Set up Node.js
        uses: actions/setup-node@v2
        with:
          node-version: '14'
      - name: Install dependencies
        run: npm install
```

```
      - name: Run tests
        run: npm test

  build:
    runs-on: ubuntu-latest
    steps:
      - name: Checkout code
        uses: actions/checkout@v2
      - name: Set up Node.js
        uses: actions/setup-node@v2
        with:
          node-version: '14'
      - name: Install dependencies
        run: npm install
      - name: Build project
        run: npm run build
```

This workflow has three jobs:

1. **Lint**: Runs ESLint to check for linting issues.
2. **Test**: Runs tests to ensure that your code behaves as expected.
3. **Build**: Builds the project using your build script (typically `npm run build`).

6.5.2 Committing the Workflow

Now commit and push the `.github/workflows/ci.yml` file to your repository. On every push or pull request to the `main` branch, GitHub Actions will automatically trigger the workflow, running the linting, testing, and build processes.

Conclusion

In this chapter, we've covered essential tooling, linting, and formatting techniques for TypeScript projects. From crafting a solid `tsconfig.json` to integrating ESLint and Prettier, and automating workflows with GitHub Actions, these tools will help you maintain clean, consistent, and error-free code.

The hands-on project demonstrates how to configure a complete CI/CD pipeline that lints, tests, and builds your project automatically, ensuring that code quality is upheld throughout the development process. With these tools and practices in place, you'll be able to develop more efficiently, catch bugs earlier, and improve collaboration across your team.

Chapter 7: Testing Strategies for Type Safety

7.1 Introduction to Testing in TypeScript

Testing is a critical part of the software development process. Writing tests ensures that your code works correctly and behaves as expected, even as you introduce new changes or refactor existing code.

```
63
64    describe('makeParagraph', () => {
65      it('Should return an HTML paragraph object', () => {
66        expect(makeParagraph('foo').tagName).toEqual('P');
67      });
68
69      it('Should render an empty paragraph, if not text provided', () => {
70        expect(makeParagraph().textContent).toEqual('');
71      });
72
73      it('Should render the correct paragraph text', () => {
74        const text = faker.lorem.sentences(3);
75        expect(makeParagraph(text).textContent).toEqual(text);
76      });
77    });
78
```

In TypeScript, testing presents an added challenge: we want to ensure that the code is not only **functional** but also **type-safe**, meaning it adheres to the types defined in the code. This ensures that we catch potential bugs and type mismatches before they make their way into production.

In this chapter, we'll explore the following:

1. Choosing a **test runner**.
2. Writing **type-aware tests** to leverage TypeScript's static typing.
3. Using **mocks and stubs** to simulate dependencies in tests.
4. Writing **snapshot tests** to ensure UI consistency.
5. Testing **asynchronous code** to handle real-world use cases.
6. **Hands-on**: Building a test suite for a REST client, including failure scenarios.

By the end of this chapter, you'll be able to confidently write unit tests for your TypeScript code, ensuring it's type-safe, reliable, and easy to maintain.

7.2 Choosing a Test Runner

A **test runner** is a tool that automates the process of running your tests. It takes care of executing tests, reporting results, and managing test configurations. There are several popular test runners available for TypeScript, each with its own features and ecosystem.

7.2.1 Jest

Jest is one of the most popular test runners for JavaScript and TypeScript. It's fast, easy to set up, and has a rich feature set, including:

- **Built-in mocking** and **spying** utilities.
- **Snapshot testing** for UI components.
- **Parallel test execution** for fast feedback.

To set up Jest in a TypeScript project:

1. Install Jest and TypeScript-related packages:

```bash
```

```
npm install --save-dev jest ts-jest @types/jest
```

2. Create a `jest.config.js` file to configure Jest with TypeScript:

```javascript
module.exports = {
  preset: 'ts-jest',
  testEnvironment: 'node',
};
```

3. Add a test script to `package.json`:

```json
"scripts": {
  "test": "jest"
}
```

Jest is ideal for most TypeScript projects because of its simplicity, ease of setup, and comprehensive feature set.

7.2.2 Mocha

Mocha is another popular test runner, widely used in the JavaScript ecosystem. It's highly flexible, and while it doesn't have built-in mocking or assertion libraries (like Jest), it can be extended using libraries like **Chai** for assertions and **Sinon** for mocks and spies.

To set up Mocha with TypeScript:

1. Install the required dependencies:

```bash
```

```
npm install --save-dev mocha chai @types/mocha
@types/chai ts-node typescript
```

2. Create a `mocha.opts` file:

    ```bash
    bash
    ```

    ```
    --require ts-node/register
    --watch-extensions ts,tsx
    ```

3. Write tests in `.ts` files and run Mocha using the `ts-node`
    loader.

7.2.3 AVA

AVA is a minimal test runner that is fast and runs tests
concurrently. It's particularly suitable for projects that require
simple, fast testing without additional features like snapshot
testing.

To set up AVA in TypeScript:

1. Install AVA and related packages:

    ```bash
    bash
    ```

    ```
    npm install --save-dev ava typescript ts-node
    ```

2. Create an `ava.config.js` file:

    ```javascript
    javascript

    export default {
      files: ['test/**/*.test.ts'],
      require: ['ts-node/register'],
    };
    ```

3. Add a test script to `package.json`:

```json
"scripts": {
  "test": "ava"
}
```

7.3 Writing Type-Aware Tests

One of the strengths of TypeScript is its **static typing**, and we can leverage that power in our tests to ensure type safety. Writing type-aware tests ensures that TypeScript catches errors at compile time, helping to avoid issues like passing incorrect data to functions or receiving unexpected return values.

7.3.1 Type Safety with Jest

When writing tests with Jest, TypeScript will infer the types of the variables you define, helping ensure your tests are type-safe.

```typescript
function add(a: number, b: number): number {
  return a + b;
}

test('adds two numbers', () => {
  const result = add(1, 2);
  expect(result).toBe(3);  // TypeScript ensures
'result' is of type 'number'
});
```

In this example:

- TypeScript ensures that the `result` is inferred as a `number`.
- If you were to accidentally pass a string to the `add()` function, TypeScript would raise an error before the test runs.

7.3.2 Using Mocks and Stubs

Mocks and stubs allow you to simulate external dependencies and isolate the code being tested. This is especially useful when dealing with **external APIs**, **database calls**, or other services that you don't want to call during unit tests.

Here's how you can use **Jest mocks** for type-safe mocking:

```typescript
// Example of a function that makes an API call
async function fetchData(url: string):
Promise<string> {
  const response = await fetch(url);
  return await response.text();
}

jest.mock('node-fetch'); // Mock the fetch module

const mockFetch = require('node-fetch');  // Import
the mock

mockFetch.mockResolvedValueOnce({ text: () => 'Hello,
world!' });  // Mock fetch's response

test('fetches data from the API', async () => {
  const result = await
fetchData('https://api.example.com');
  expect(result).toBe('Hello, world!');
});
```

In this example:

- We mock the `fetch` function using Jest's `jest.mock()` method.
- TypeScript ensures the return types of mocked functions are compatible with what is expected.

7.3.3 Type Safety with Mocha

If you're using Mocha, you can still benefit from TypeScript's type checking. Here's how you can write type-safe tests with Mocha and Chai:

```typescript
import { expect } from 'chai';

function multiply(a: number, b: number): number {
  return a * b;
}

describe('multiply function', () => {
  it('should multiply two numbers', () => {
    const result = multiply(2, 3);
    expect(result).to.equal(6);  // TypeScript
ensures 'result' is of type 'number'
  });
});
```

Mocha doesn't come with built-in type safety, but TypeScript's static analysis works seamlessly with it, catching type-related issues as you write tests.

7.4 Snapshot Testing and Testing Async Code

7.4.1 Snapshot Testing

Snapshot testing is a powerful feature provided by Jest that allows you to capture the output of a function, component, or module and compare it to a reference snapshot. If the output changes unexpectedly, Jest will notify you that the snapshot has changed, which helps you detect unintended side effects.

Here's an example of how to use snapshot testing with Jest:

```typescript
```

```typescript
import { formatDate } from './utils';

test('formats the date correctly', () => {
  const result = formatDate(new Date(2021, 0, 1));
  expect(result).toMatchSnapshot();  // Jest takes a
snapshot of the result
});
```

In this example:

- The `formatDate` function is tested to ensure it formats the date correctly.
- Jest will take a snapshot of the result the first time the test runs and compare it to future runs.

7.4.2 Testing Async Code

Testing asynchronous code can be tricky, but TypeScript's type system makes it easier to ensure that your promises or async functions return the expected types.

With **Jest**, you can test async code using `async/await` or `done`:

typescript

```typescript
async function fetchData(url: string):
Promise<string> {
  const response = await fetch(url);
  return await response.text();
}

test('fetches data from an API asynchronously', async
() => {
  const result = await
fetchData('https://api.example.com');
  expect(result).toBe('Hello, world!');
});
```

- Jest will automatically handle the promise returned by `fetchData`, and TypeScript ensures that `result` is of type `string`.

For Mocha, you can use the `done` callback to handle async tests:

```typescript
import { expect } from 'chai';

async function fetchData(url: string):
Promise<string> {
  const response = await fetch(url);
  return response.text();
}

it('should fetch data asynchronously', (done) => {
  fetchData('https://api.example.com')
    .then(result => {
      expect(result).to.equal('Hello, world!');
      done();
    })
    .catch(done);
});
```

Here, `done` signals that the test has completed, ensuring Mocha knows when to stop waiting for the asynchronous operation to finish.

7.5 Hands-On: Building a Test Suite for a REST Client

In this hands-on section, we will create a **test suite for a REST client** using **Jest**. The client will fetch data from an API, and we'll write tests to handle both successful and failure scenarios.

7.5.1 Creating the REST Client

Let's create a simple REST client that fetches data from a mock API:

typescript

```typescript
import fetch from 'node-fetch';

export async function fetchData(url: string):
Promise<any> {
  const response = await fetch(url);
  if (!response.ok) {
    throw new Error('Network response was not ok');
  }
  return response.json();
}
```

7.5.2 Writing Tests for the REST Client

Now, let's write tests for this client, including handling both success and failure scenarios.

typescript

```typescript
import { fetchData } from './fetchData';
import fetch from 'node-fetch';

jest.mock('node-fetch');
const { Response } = jest.requireActual('node-fetch');

test('fetches data successfully', async () => {
  const mockResponse = { message: 'Hello, world!' };
  fetch.mockResolvedValueOnce(new
Response(JSON.stringify(mockResponse), { status: 200
})));

  const data = await
fetchData('https://api.example.com');
  expect(data).toEqual(mockResponse);
});
```

```
test('throws error when network response is not ok',
async () => {
  fetch.mockResolvedValueOnce(new Response(null, {
status: 500 }));

  await
expect(fetchData('https://api.example.com')).rejects.
toThrow('Network response was not ok');
});
```

- In the **first test**, we mock a successful response from the API and ensure the client returns the correct data.
- In the **second test**, we simulate a network error by returning a failed HTTP status code, and verify that the client throws the appropriate error.

Conclusion

In this chapter, we covered **testing strategies** for TypeScript applications, focusing on ensuring **type safety** throughout your tests. We explored:

1. Choosing the right **test runner** like Jest, Mocha, or AVA for your needs.
2. Writing **type-aware tests** that leverage TypeScript's static typing to prevent bugs.
3. Using **mocks and stubs** to simulate external dependencies and isolate units of code.
4. Implementing **snapshot testing** for UI consistency and **testing async code** effectively.
5. Building a comprehensive **test suite** for a REST client, handling both success and failure scenarios.

By integrating these testing strategies into your workflow, you'll ensure your TypeScript code is both reliable and type-safe, ultimately leading to a more maintainable and bug-free application.

Chapter 8: Integrating with Frontend Frameworks

8.1 Introduction to Integrating TypeScript with Frontend Frameworks

TypeScript is the ideal companion for modern frontend frameworks. With its static typing and support for modern JavaScript features, TypeScript enhances the development experience by providing **early error detection**, **better IDE support**, and **improved refactoring** capabilities.

Each frontend framework has its unique approach to building user interfaces, managing state, and structuring applications. By integrating TypeScript, you can improve the maintainability and scalability of your projects, whether you're building **small widgets** or **large, complex applications**.

In this chapter, we'll dive deep into how TypeScript works with popular frontend frameworks like **React**, **Angular**, **Vue**, and **Svelte**. We'll cover:

1. **React**: Managing props, state, hooks, and context in TypeScript.
2. **Angular**: Using strict templates and dependency injection with TypeScript.
3. **Vue** and **Svelte**: Integrating TypeScript in these modern frameworks.
4. **Hands-on**: Developing a small **React component library** with typed props and publishing it to a private npm registry.

8.2 React: Props, State, Hooks, and Context in TypeScript

React is a popular frontend library for building user interfaces. It's highly component-based, meaning you can create reusable pieces of UI, which makes React a great fit for **type-safe** development with TypeScript.

8.2.1 Working with Props in TypeScript

In React, **props** are used to pass data into components. TypeScript allows you to define the shape of these props, ensuring that components receive the right type of data.

Here's an example of defining **typed props** in a functional component:

```tsx
interface GreetingProps {
  name: string;
  age: number;
}

const Greeting: React.FC<GreetingProps> = ({ name,
age }) => {
  return <div>Hello, {name}! You are {age} years
old.</div>;
};

// Usage
<Greeting name="Alice" age={30} />;
```

- In this example:
    - We define an interface `GreetingProps` to specify the expected props for the `Greeting` component.
    - `name` is a `string`, and `age` is a `number`. TypeScript ensures that only the correct types can be passed to the component.

8.2.2 Managing State in TypeScript

React provides a `useState` hook to manage state within functional components. TypeScript can infer the type of the state variable, but it's often beneficial to explicitly define the type.

Here's how you can define typed state using `useState`:

tsx

```tsx
const [count, setCount] = useState<number>(0);

const increment = () => setCount(count + 1);

return (
  <div>
    <p>Count: {count}</p>
    <button onClick={increment}>Increment</button>
  </div>
);
```

- `useState<number>(0)` explicitly tells TypeScript that `count` is a `number`.
- TypeScript ensures that `count` remains a `number` and that `setCount` only accepts numbers.

8.2.3 Using Hooks with TypeScript

React's hooks like `useEffect`, `useReducer`, and `useContext` are powerful tools for managing side effects, complex state, and shared data. With TypeScript, you can use these hooks with the appropriate types for your application.

Example of using `useEffect` with TypeScript:

tsx

```tsx
import { useState, useEffect } from 'react';

const DataFetcher: React.FC = () => {
```

```
  const [data, setData] = useState<string |
null>(null);

  useEffect(() => {
    fetch('/api/data')
      .then((res) => res.json())
      .then((data) => setData(data));
  }, []); // Empty array means this effect runs only
once when the component mounts

  return <div>{data ? data : "Loading..."}</div>;
};
```

- **Here,** `useState<string | null>(null)` **specifies that** `data` **can either be a** `string` **or** `null`.
- `useEffect` **is used to fetch data asynchronously, and TypeScript ensures the correct types are used.**

8.2.4 Using Context API with TypeScript

The **Context API** in React allows you to share state across components without passing props manually through every level of the tree.

Example of using **React Context** with TypeScript:

```tsx
tsx

interface UserContextType {
  user: string;
  setUser: (user: string) => void;
}

const UserContext =
React.createContext<UserContextType |
undefined>(undefined);

const UserProvider: React.FC = ({ children }) => {
  const [user, setUser] = useState<string>('John
Doe');
  return (
```

```
    <UserContext.Provider value={{ user, setUser }}>
      {children}
    </UserContext.Provider>
  );
};

const UserProfile: React.FC = () => {
  const context = useContext(UserContext);
  if (!context) {
    throw new Error("useContext must be used within a
UserProvider");
  }

  return <div>Welcome, {context.user}!</div>;
};
```

- `React.createContext<UserContextType |
  undefined>(undefined)` creates a context with an initial
  value of `undefined` and expects the context to provide
  both the `user` and a `setUser` function.
- TypeScript ensures that the `UserContext` is used correctly
  and catches errors when the context is not provided.

8.3 Angular: Strict Templates and Dependency Injection with TypeScript

Angular is a full-fledged framework that provides a comprehensive approach to building applications. It uses **dependency injection (DI)** for managing services and **strict templates** to ensure type safety throughout the app.

8.3.1 Strict Templates in Angular

Angular's **strict templates** ensure that your HTML templates are type-safe and properly integrated with your TypeScript code. This means TypeScript ensures that the variables and functions you reference in your templates are defined and correctly typed.

Here's an example:

typescript

```typescript
@Component({
  selector: 'app-greeting',
  template: '<h1>Hello, {{ name }}!</h1>',
})
export class GreetingComponent {
  name: string = 'Alice';
}
```

- In the template, `{{ name }}` is automatically bound to the `name` property of the component.
- TypeScript ensures that `name` is a `string`, so you can't accidentally bind a variable of the wrong type in the template.

8.3.2 Dependency Injection in Angular

Angular uses **dependency injection (DI)** to provide services to components and other parts of the application. DI ensures that dependencies are injected into classes rather than being manually instantiated.

Here's an example of using DI in an Angular service:

typescript

```typescript
@Injectable({
  providedIn: 'root',
})
export class UserService {
  getUser(): string {
    return 'John Doe';
  }
}

@Component({
  selector: 'app-user',
  template: '<div>{{ user }}</div>',
```

```
})
export class UserComponent {
  user: string;

  constructor(private userService: UserService) {
    this.user = this.userService.getUser();
  }
}
```

- The `UserService` is injected into the `UserComponent` through the constructor.
- TypeScript ensures that `UserService` is correctly injected and that the types match.

8.4 Vue and Svelte: Basics with TypeScript

Both **Vue** and **Svelte** are modern frameworks that are highly compatible with TypeScript. Let's explore how to integrate TypeScript with each.

8.4.1 Vue with TypeScript

Vue 3 has excellent support for TypeScript. It provides **type-safe props**, **ref bindings**, and **computed properties**.

Here's an example of a typed Vue component:

```typescript
<template>
  <div>{{ message }}</div>
</template>

<script lang="ts">
import { defineComponent, ref } from 'vue';

export default defineComponent({
  props: {
    message: {
```

```
      type: String,
      required: true,
    },
  },
  setup() {
    const count = ref(0);
    return { count };
  },
});
</script>
```

- The `message` prop is defined with its type, ensuring that Vue will expect a string.
- `ref(0)` is used to define a reactive variable with type `number`.

8.4.2 Svelte with TypeScript

Svelte also supports TypeScript out of the box, though you must enable TypeScript in the Svelte configuration. Here's a simple example of a typed Svelte component:

```svelte
<script lang="ts">
  export let name: string;
</script>

<h1>Hello, {name}!</h1>
```

- In this example, `name` is typed as a `string` and passed as a prop to the component.
- TypeScript ensures that `name` is always a string, providing type safety throughout the application.

8.5 Hands-On: Developing a React Component Library with Typed Props

In this hands-on section, we'll develop a small **React component library** with typed props, which can be published to a **private npm registry**.

8.5.1 Setting Up the Project

1. Create a new directory for your component library:

   bash

   ```
   mkdir react-component-library
   cd react-component-library
   ```

2. Initialize a new **npm** project:

   bash

   ```
   npm init -y
   ```

3. Install necessary dependencies:

   bash

   ```
   npm install react react-dom
   npm install --save-dev typescript @types/react
   @types/react-dom
   ```

4. Create a `tsconfig.json` file to configure TypeScript for the library:

   json

   ```
   {
     "compilerOptions": {
       "target": "es5",
       "module": "esnext",
       "declaration": true,
   ```

```
    "outDir": "./dist",
    "jsx": "react-jsx"
  },
  "include": ["src/**/*.tsx"]
}
```

8.5.2 Building a Simple Button Component

Create a `src/Button.tsx` file for a simple button component with typed props:

tsx

```tsx
import React from 'react';

interface ButtonProps {
  label: string;
  onClick: () => void;
}

const Button: React.FC<ButtonProps> = ({ label,
onClick }) => {
  return <button onClick={onClick}>{label}</button>;
};

export default Button;
```

- The `Button` component accepts a `label` (string) and an `onClick` function as props.

8.5.3 Packaging and Publishing the Library

1. Compile the TypeScript code:

   bash

   ```bash
   npx tsc
   ```

2. To publish the component library to a private npm registry, you'll need to configure your `.npmrc` file to point to the private registry.

3. Publish the package:

```bash
npm publish --access=restricted
```

Now, your React component library is ready to be used across different projects with type safety provided by TypeScript!

Conclusion

In this chapter, we explored how to integrate **TypeScript** with **React, Angular, Vue**, and **Svelte** to create type-safe, scalable frontend applications. We covered key concepts like **props, state, hooks, context**, and **dependency injection**, while demonstrating how to write type-safe components in each framework.

The **hands-on project** guided you through creating a simple **React component library**, which was then packaged and published to a private npm registry. This workflow ensures that your components are reusable, maintainable, and type-safe.

By mastering TypeScript with these frontend frameworks, you can ensure that your applications are built with maintainability and type safety at the forefront, enabling better collaboration and fewer runtime errors.

Chapter 9: Building Typed Backends with Node.js

9.1 Introduction to Backend Development with TypeScript

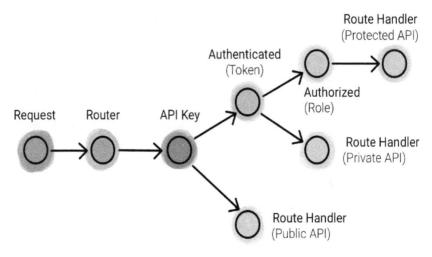

In backend development, building type-safe APIs is crucial for ensuring that your application behaves correctly as it scales. TypeScript's **static typing** enables developers to catch errors early, making applications more reliable and easier to maintain. In this chapter, we'll explore how to build **typed backends** with **Node.js**, focusing on the following key areas:

1. **Express** and **Koa** frameworks, and their integration with **decorator-based routing**.
2. Typing **request payloads** and **responses** for better type safety.
3. **Data validation** techniques using **Zod** or **Yup** for ensuring that incoming data matches the expected format.

4. **Hands-on**: Building a **CRUD API server** that validates input and responds with typed DTOs.

By the end of this chapter, you will understand how to implement type-safe routes, ensure proper data validation, and work with typed request and response objects in Node.js applications.

9.2 Express and Koa with Decorator-Based Routing

Node.js has a rich ecosystem of web frameworks that help simplify the creation of APIs. **Express** is the most widely used backend framework for Node.js, but **Koa** (also developed by the creators of Express) offers a more minimalistic and flexible approach.

9.2.1 Setting Up Express with TypeScript

To get started with **Express** in TypeScript, you need to install the required dependencies:

bash

```
npm install express
npm install --save-dev typescript @types/express
```

Then, create a `tsconfig.json` file to configure TypeScript for the Express app:

json

```
{
  "compilerOptions": {
    "target": "es6",
    "module": "commonjs",
    "strict": true,
    "esModuleInterop": true,
    "skipLibCheck": true,
```

```
    "forceConsistentCasingInFileNames": true,
    "outDir": "./dist",
    "rootDir": "./src"
  },
  "include": ["src/**/*.ts"]
}
```

Create a simple **Express server** with TypeScript:

```typescript
import express, { Request, Response } from "express";

const app = express();
const port = 3000;

app.get("/", (req: Request, res: Response) => {
  res.send("Hello, World!");
});

app.listen(port, () => {
  console.log(`Server is running on
http://localhost:${port}`);
});
```

In this setup:

- TypeScript ensures type safety for `Request` and `Response` objects, making the development process smoother by providing autocompletion and type checks.

9.2.2 Koa with TypeScript

While Express is very popular, **Koa** offers more flexibility and a smaller footprint, giving developers greater control over the request/response cycle. To set up **Koa** with TypeScript, install the following dependencies:

```bash
```

```
npm install koa
npm install --save-dev typescript @types/koa
```

Here's a simple **Koa server** setup:

```typescript
import Koa from "koa";
import Router from "@koa/router";

const app = new Koa();
const router = new Router();

router.get("/", async (ctx) => {
  ctx.body = "Hello, Koa!";
});

app
    .use(router.routes())
    .use(router.allowedMethods());

app.listen(3000, () => {
  console.log("Koa server is running on
http://localhost:3000");
});
```

In this setup:

- `@koa/router` is used to define routes, and Koa provides more fine-grained control over request handling.
- We also have the benefits of TypeScript's type inference to ensure proper typing in the routes.

9.2.3 Decorator-Based Routing

Decorator-based routing is an advanced feature where decorators are used to define routes and middleware in a more **declarative** manner. Libraries like **TypeORM** and **InversifyJS** support decorators, but **routing-controllers** makes this pattern especially useful in **Express** and **Koa**.

To use **decorator-based routing**, you can use the `routing-controllers` library:

bash

```
npm install routing-controllers reflect-metadata
npm install --save-dev @types/express
```

In your `tsconfig.json`, enable the experimental decorators and metadata reflection:

json

```
{
  "compilerOptions": {
    "experimentalDecorators": true,
    "emitDecoratorMetadata": true
  }
}
```

Here's an example using **routing-controllers** in Express:

typescript

```
import { Controller, Get } from "routing-controllers";
import express from "express";
import { useExpressServer } from "routing-controllers";

@Controller()
class MyController {
  @Get()
  getHello(): string {
    return "Hello from TypeScript with decorators!";
  }
}

const app = express();
useExpressServer(app, {
  controllers: [MyController]
});
```

```
app.listen(3000, () => {
  console.log("Server is running with decorators!");
});
```

In this example:

- The @Controller decorator defines a controller class, and the @Get decorator defines the GET route.
- **TypeScript** ensures that the parameters and return types are correctly typed, providing type safety and improved readability.

9.3 Typing Request Payloads and Responses

One of the biggest benefits of using **TypeScript** in backend development is the ability to define **types for request payloads** (data sent in HTTP requests) and **response bodies** (data returned by the server).

9.3.1 Typing Request Payloads

In a **REST API**, request payloads are typically sent in the body of a POST, PUT, or PATCH request. To enforce type safety for these payloads, you can define **DTOs** (Data Transfer Objects) for incoming data.

For example, let's define a CreateUserDto for a POST /users endpoint in **Express**:

```typescript
interface CreateUserDto {
  name: string;
  email: string;
}

app.post("/users", (req: Request, res: Response) => {
```

```
  const user: CreateUserDto = req.body; // TypeScript
ensures the request body matches the DTO

  res.status(201).json({
    message: "User created",
    user,
  });
});
```

- CreateUserDto ensures that the `name` and `email` fields are present in the request payload, with the correct types.

9.3.2 Typing Responses

It's also important to ensure that responses are properly typed. You can define a type for the response body and return it within the route handler:

```typescript
interface UserResponseDto {
  id: string;
  name: string;
  email: string;
}

app.get("/users/:id", (req: Request, res: Response)
=> {
  const user: UserResponseDto = {
    id: req.params.id,
    name: "John Doe",
    email: "john@example.com",
  };

  res.status(200).json(user); // TypeScript ensures
the response body matches the DTO
});
```

- UserResponseDto ensures that the response contains the correct fields and types, providing clarity and reducing runtime errors.

9.4 Data Validation with Zod or Yup

Data validation is crucial in any backend application to ensure that the data being processed is correct, secure, and well-structured. **Zod** and **Yup** are two popular validation libraries that work seamlessly with TypeScript.

9.4.1 Using Zod for Data Validation

Zod is a TypeScript-first validation library that makes it easy to define schemas for data validation. Zod automatically infers types from your validation schemas, which ensures that your types are always in sync with your validation logic.

Here's how to use **Zod** for input validation:

1. Install Zod:

    bash

    ```bash
    npm install zod
    ```

2. Define a `CreateUserDto` schema using Zod:

    typescript

    ```typescript
    import { z } from "zod";

    const CreateUserDto = z.object({
      name: z.string().min(1),
      email: z.string().email(),
    });

    type CreateUserDtoType = z.infer<typeof CreateUserDto>;
    ```

3. Use Zod to validate the request payload:

```typescript
app.post("/users", (req: Request, res:
Response) => {
  try {
    const user: CreateUserDtoType =
CreateUserDto.parse(req.body); // Validates and
types the request
    res.status(201).json({
      message: "User created",
      user,
    });
  } catch (error) {
    res.status(400).json({
      message: "Invalid data",
      error: error.errors,
    });
  }
});
```

- **Zod** validates the request body and ensures that the incoming data matches the schema.
- If validation fails, the `catch` block returns an appropriate error response.

9.4.2 Using Yup for Data Validation

Yup is another powerful validation library that works well with TypeScript. While it's slightly more verbose than Zod, it's widely used and integrates well with other libraries.

To use **Yup** for validation:

1. Install Yup:

   ```bash
   npm install yup
   ```

2. Define a `CreateUserDto` schema:

```typescript
import * as yup from "yup";

const CreateUserDto = yup.object({
  name: yup.string().required().min(1),
  email: yup.string().email().required(),
});

type CreateUserDtoType = yup.InferType<typeof
CreateUserDto>;
```

3. Validate the request payload using Yup:

```typescript
app.post("/users", async (req: Request, res:
Response) => {
  try {
    const user: CreateUserDtoType = await
CreateUserDto.validate(req.body); // Validates
the data
    res.status(201).json({
      message: "User created",
      user,
    });
  } catch (error) {
    res.status(400).json({
      message: "Invalid data",
      error: error.errors,
    });
  }
});
```

- **Yup** works similarly to Zod but with a more flexible API for validation and error handling.

9.5 Hands-On: Creating a CRUD API Server with Typed DTOs and Data Validation

Let's now build a simple **CRUD API server** using **Express**, **Zod** for data validation, and **TypeScript** for type safety.

9.5.1 Setting Up the Project

1. Initialize a new Node.js project:

    bash

    ```
    mkdir express-crud-api
    cd express-crud-api
    npm init -y
    ```

2. Install the necessary dependencies:

    bash

    ```
    npm install express zod
    npm install --save-dev typescript
    @types/express @types/node
    ```

3. Set up the `tsconfig.json` file as we did earlier in the chapter.

9.5.2 Defining DTOs and Schemas

We'll define a `CreateUserDto` schema using **Zod** for validation and ensure that the request body is properly typed:

typescript

```typescript
import { z } from "zod";

// DTO Schema
const CreateUserDto = z.object({
  name: z.string().min(1),
```

```typescript
  email: z.string().email(),
});

type CreateUserDtoType = z.infer<typeof
CreateUserDto>;
```

9.5.3 Setting Up CRUD Routes

Now, let's create the CRUD routes for the API:

```typescript
import express, { Request, Response } from "express";

const app = express();
app.use(express.json());

// In-memory database for users (for simplicity)
const users: CreateUserDtoType[] = [];

// Create User
app.post("/users", (req: Request, res: Response) => {
  try {
    const user: CreateUserDtoType =
CreateUserDto.parse(req.body); // Validates and types
the request
    users.push(user);
    res.status(201).json(user);
  } catch (error) {
    res.status(400).json({
      message: "Invalid data",
      error: error.errors,
    });
  }
});

// Get all users
app.get("/users", (req: Request, res: Response) => {
  res.json(users);
});

// Get user by ID
```

```
app.get("/users/:id", (req: Request, res: Response)
=> {
  const user = users[parseInt(req.params.id)];
  if (!user) {
    res.status(404).json({ message: "User not found"
});
  } else {
    res.json(user);
  }
});

// Update user by ID
app.put("/users/:id", (req: Request, res: Response)
=> {
  try {
    const user: CreateUserDtoType =
CreateUserDto.parse(req.body); // Validates and types
the request
    const index = parseInt(req.params.id);
    if (!users[index]) {
      res.status(404).json({ message: "User not
found" });
    } else {
      users[index] = user;
      res.json(user);
    }
  } catch (error) {
    res.status(400).json({
      message: "Invalid data",
      error: error.errors,
    });
  }
});

// Delete user by ID
app.delete("/users/:id", (req: Request, res:
Response) => {
  const index = parseInt(req.params.id);
  if (users[index]) {
    users.splice(index, 1);
    res.status(204).send();
  } else {
    res.status(404).json({ message: "User not found"
});
```

```
  }
});

app.listen(3000, () => {
  console.log("Server is running on
http://localhost:3000");
});
```

9.5.4 Testing the API

You can test the API using **Postman** or **Insomnia**. Here's a
summary of the routes:

- `POST /users`: Creates a new user (requires `name` and
  `email`).
- `GET /users`: Fetches all users.
- `GET /users/:id`: Fetches a user by ID.
- `PUT /users/:id`: Updates a user by ID (requires `name`
  and `email`).
- `DELETE /users/:id`: Deletes a user by ID.

Conclusion

In this chapter, we learned how to build **typed backends** with
Node.js and **TypeScript**. We explored:

1. Using **Express** and **Koa** to create type-safe routes.
2. Typing **request payloads** and **responses** to ensure that
   the correct data types are used throughout the application.
3. Validating incoming data with **Zod** and **Yup** to ensure that
   our backend handles only valid data.
4. **Hands-on**: Creating a **CRUD API** with **Express** that
   validates input and responds with typed DTOs.

By integrating TypeScript into your backend workflow, you can
write safer, more maintainable, and scalable code that benefits
from TypeScript's **type checking** and **data validation** features.

Chapter 10: Working with Datastores and APIs

10.1 Introduction to Working with Datastores and APIs

In modern web development, applications often need to interact with **datastores** (databases) to persist data, as well as consume external **APIs** (Application Programming Interfaces) to access remote resources or services.

TypeScript makes working with both **databases** and **APIs** easier and safer by providing **static types** that ensure data integrity throughout the development process. By leveraging **Object-Relational Mappers (ORMs)** like **TypeORM** and **Prisma** for SQL/NoSQL databases, as well as auto-generating **types** for **REST** or **GraphQL APIs**, we can build more robust applications while reducing the likelihood of runtime errors.

In this chapter, we will focus on the following areas:

1. Using **ORMS** like **TypeORM** and **Prisma** to manage **SQL** and **NoSQL** databases in TypeScript.
2. **Auto-generating TypeScript types** from **OpenAPI** or **GraphQL** schemas.
3. **Consuming third-party REST and GraphQL services** with **type safety**.
4. **Hands-on**: Auto-generate types from an OpenAPI spec and call the API with full type safety.

10.2 Using ORMs for SQL and NoSQL Databases

10.2.1 Introduction to ORMs

An **Object-Relational Mapper (ORM)** is a tool that allows developers to interact with a database using **objects** in their programming language, rather than writing raw SQL queries. With TypeScript, using an ORM helps ensure type safety when interacting with databases, making it easier to define and query the database schema.

Two of the most popular ORMs for Node.js are **TypeORM** and **Prisma**. Let's explore both of them in detail.

10.2.2 Using TypeORM with TypeScript

TypeORM is an ORM for **SQL databases** (like MySQL, PostgreSQL, SQLite, etc.). It integrates seamlessly with TypeScript and provides an easy-to-use interface for interacting with the database.

10.2.2.1 Setting Up TypeORM

1. Install TypeORM and the required database driver (e.g., for PostgreSQL):

   bash

   ```
   npm install typeorm pg
   npm install --save-dev typescript @types/node
   ```

2. Create a `tsconfig.json` file to enable TypeScript compilation:

   json

   ```
   {
     "compilerOptions": {
       "target": "ES6",
       "module": "commonjs",
   ```

```json
    "strict": true,
    "esModuleInterop": true,
    "skipLibCheck": true,
    "forceConsistentCasingInFileNames": true,
    "outDir": "./dist",
    "rootDir": "./src"
  },
  "include": ["src/**/*.ts"]
}
```

3. Set up a basic **TypeORM** configuration (`ormconfig.json`):

json

```json
{
  "type": "postgres",
  "host": "localhost",
  "port": 5432,
  "username": "test",
  "password": "test",
  "database": "test_db",
  "entities": ["src/entity/*.ts"],
  "synchronize": true
}
```

4. Create an **entity** (database model):

typescript

```typescript
import { Entity, PrimaryGeneratedColumn, Column } from "typeorm";

@Entity()
export class User {
  @PrimaryGeneratedColumn()
  id: number;

  @Column()
  name: string;

  @Column()
  email: string;
}
```

5. Create a simple **TypeORM** connection and save data:

```typescript
import "reflect-metadata";
import { createConnection } from "typeorm";
import { User } from "./entity/User";

createConnection().then(async connection => {
  const userRepository =
connection.getRepository(User);
  const user = new User();
  user.name = "Alice";
  user.email = "alice@example.com";
  await userRepository.save(user);
  console.log("User saved:", user);
}).catch(error => console.log(error));
```

In this example:

- The `User` entity represents a table in the database with columns `id`, `name`, and `email`.
- TypeORM automatically handles SQL query generation for inserting and querying the `User` table, while TypeScript ensures that the properties of `User` match the expected types.

10.2.3 Using Prisma with TypeScript

Prisma is another ORM, but it provides a more modern, **type-safe** approach to working with databases. Prisma uses a **Prisma schema** to define models and supports both **SQL** and **NoSQL** databases.

10.2.3.1 Setting Up Prisma

1. Install Prisma and the database client:

```bash
bash

npm install prisma @prisma/client
```

2. Initialize Prisma:

```bash
bash

npx prisma init
```

3. Define your **Prisma schema** in `prisma/schema.prisma`:

```prisma
prisma

datasource db {
  provider = "postgresql"
  url      = env("DATABASE_URL")
}

generator client {
  provider = "prisma-client-js"
}

model User {
  id    Int     @id @default(autoincrement())
  name  String
  email String @unique
}
```

4. Generate Prisma Client and apply migrations:

```bash
bash

npx prisma migrate dev --name init
npx prisma generate
```

5. Interact with the database using Prisma Client in your TypeScript code:

```typescript
import { PrismaClient } from '@prisma/client';

const prisma = new PrismaClient();

async function main() {
  const user = await prisma.user.create({
    data: {
      name: 'Alice',
      email: 'alice@example.com',
    },
  });
  console.log(user);
}

main()
  .catch(e => {
    throw e;
  })
  .finally(async () => {
    await prisma.$disconnect();
  });
```

In this example:

- **Prisma** generates a type-safe client based on the schema, ensuring that you can only query and mutate the database using valid model names and fields.

10.3 Generating TypeScript Types from OpenAPI or GraphQL Schemas

One of the most powerful features TypeScript offers is **type safety**, which can be extended to external APIs. By auto-generating types from **OpenAPI** or **GraphQL** schemas, you can ensure that the data you send to or receive from an API adheres to the expected structure.

10.3.1 Generating Types from OpenAPI Specifications

OpenAPI (formerly known as Swagger) is a specification for building and consuming REST APIs. By using **OpenAPI schemas**, you can automatically generate **TypeScript types** for the API responses and requests.

10.3.1.1 Setting Up OpenAPI Codegen

You can use the **OpenAPI Generator** to auto-generate TypeScript types from an OpenAPI spec:

1. Install the OpenAPI Generator:

   bash

   ```
   npm install @openapitools/openapi-generator-cli
   --save-dev
   ```

2. Generate TypeScript client from an OpenAPI spec:

   bash

   ```
   npx openapi-generator-cli generate -i
   https://api.example.com/openapi.json -g
   typescript-fetch -o ./generated-api
   ```

This command generates a TypeScript client based on the OpenAPI specification.

10.3.1.2 Using Generated Types

You can then use the generated types in your application:

typescript

```
import { ApiClient, GetUserResponse } from
'./generated-api';

const client = new ApiClient();
```

```
async function getUser(id: string):
Promise<GetUserResponse> {
  const response = await client.getUserById({ userId:
id });
  return response.data;
}
```

- The `GetUserResponse` type is auto-generated from the OpenAPI schema, ensuring that the API response matches the expected structure.

10.3.2 Generating Types from GraphQL Schemas

GraphQL is a query language for APIs, and like OpenAPI, GraphQL schemas can be used to auto-generate TypeScript types.

10.3.2.1 Setting Up Apollo Client with TypeScript

1. Install Apollo Client and its TypeScript dependencies:

   bash

   ```
   npm install @apollo/client graphql
   npm install --save-dev @graphql-codegen/cli
   ```

2. Set up **GraphQL Code Generator** to auto-generate TypeScript types:

   bash

   ```
   npx graphql-codegen init
   ```

3. Generate types from the GraphQL schema:

   bash

   ```
   npx graphql-codegen
   ```

10.3.2.2 Using Generated Types

Once the types are generated, you can use them in your application:

typescript

```typescript
import { useQuery } from '@apollo/client';
import { GetUserQuery, GetUserQueryVariables } from
'./generated/graphql';

const GET_USER = gql`
  query GetUser($id: ID!) {
    user(id: $id) {
      id
      name
    }
  }
`;

function getUser(id: string): Promise<GetUserQuery> {
  const { data } = useQuery<GetUserQuery,
GetUserQueryVariables>(GET_USER, {
    variables: { id },
  });

  return data;
}
```

- The generated types ensure that both the query and the response data match the GraphQL schema, providing type safety when interacting with the API.

10.4 Consuming Third-Party REST and GraphQL Services

Once you have auto-generated types for **REST** or **GraphQL** APIs, consuming third-party services becomes straightforward and type-safe. You can use these types to ensure the API data matches the expected structure.

10.4.1 Consuming a REST API

When consuming a REST API, it's essential to ensure that the data returned by the API is correctly typed.

typescript

```typescript
import axios from 'axios';
import { UserResponseDto } from './types';

async function fetchUserData(userId: string):
Promise<UserResponseDto> {
  const response = await
axios.get<UserResponseDto>(`https://api.example.com/u
sers/${userId}`);
  return response.data;
}
```

- By specifying the type `<UserResponseDto>` when making the request, TypeScript ensures that the returned data matches the `UserResponseDto` type, providing automatic type checks.

10.4.2 Consuming a GraphQL API

For **GraphQL** APIs, you can use the `Apollo Client` to interact with the service and benefit from **type-safe queries**.

typescript

```typescript
import { ApolloClient, InMemoryCache, gql } from
'@apollo/client';
import { GetUserQuery } from './generated/graphql';

const client = new ApolloClient({
  uri: 'https://api.example.com/graphql',
  cache: new InMemoryCache(),
});
```

```
const GET_USER = gql`
  query GetUser($id: ID!) {
    user(id: $id) {
      id
      name
    }
  }
`;

async function fetchUser(id: string):
Promise<GetUserQuery> {
  const { data } = await client.query<GetUserQuery>({
    query: GET_USER,
    variables: { id },
  });

  return data;
}
```

- In this example, the `GetUserQuery` type is generated from the GraphQL schema, ensuring that both the query and the response data are type-safe.

10.5 Hands-On: Auto-Generate Types from an OpenAPI Spec

Now, let's walk through a **hands-on** project where we auto-generate types from an **OpenAPI spec** and use these types to make type-safe API calls.

10.5.1 Setting Up the Project

1. Initialize the Node.js project:

```bash
bash
```

```bash
mkdir openapi-typescript-example
cd openapi-typescript-example
npm init -y
```

2. Install necessary dependencies:

```bash
bash

npm install axios
npm install --save-dev @openapitools/openapi-
generator-cli typescript
```

3. Generate TypeScript client from OpenAPI spec:

```bash
bash

npx openapi-generator-cli generate -i
https://api.example.com/openapi.json -g
typescript-axios -o ./generated-api
```

10.5.2 Using the Generated Types

Now that we've generated the types and client, we can use the generated code to make type-safe API calls:

```typescript
typescript

import { ApiClient, GetUserResponse } from
'./generated-api';

const apiClient = new ApiClient();

async function getUserData(userId: string):
Promise<GetUserResponse> {
  const response = await apiClient.getUserById({
userId });
  return response.data;
}
```

In this example:

- We use the generated `ApiClient` and `GetUserResponse` types to ensure type safety when interacting with the API.

Conclusion

In this chapter, we covered how to **build typed backends** and interact with **datastores** and **APIs** in TypeScript. We explored **ORMS** like **TypeORM** and **Prisma** for interacting with SQL/NoSQL databases, **auto-generating types** from **OpenAPI** and **GraphQL** schemas, and consuming third-party REST and GraphQL services with **type safety**.

The **hands-on project** demonstrated how to **auto-generate types from an OpenAPI spec** and consume the API with full type safety, ensuring your application remains maintainable and error-free.

Chapter 11: Organizing Large-Scale Codebases

11.1 Introduction to Large-Scale Codebases in TypeScript

As projects grow in size and complexity, maintaining a clean and well-organized codebase becomes essential. **TypeScript** provides powerful tools that can help manage large projects, but without the proper structure, even TypeScript's type safety can't prevent the challenges associated with large codebases.

In this chapter, we will explore strategies for organizing large-scale TypeScript codebases using:

1. **Project references** and **path aliases** to manage dependencies across different parts of a project.
2. **Monorepo setups** with tools like **Yarn Workspaces** or **pnpm** to manage multiple packages under a single repository.
3. **Sharing types** and **utilities** across multiple packages to reduce redundancy and ensure consistency.
4. A **hands-on example** to set up a two-package monorepo for managing shared types and application logic.

These strategies will help you ensure that your codebase remains maintainable, scalable, and easier to manage, especially as your project grows and new developers come on board.

11.2 Project References, Path Aliases, and Composite Projects

When working with large codebases, **project references** and **path aliases** are invaluable tools in TypeScript for organizing your code in a modular and scalable way. These techniques enable you to split your code into smaller, manageable pieces while maintaining strong type safety across modules.

11.2.1 Project References in TypeScript

Project references allow you to link different TypeScript projects together, making it easier to work with multiple modules or packages in a large project. This is particularly useful for separating concerns and enabling faster incremental builds.

To set up project references, you need to have a **tsconfig.json** for each project you want to reference. Here's how you can set up a simple project reference structure.

11.2.1.1 Creating Project References

1. Start by creating a new directory for your project and initialize a `tsconfig.json`:

   bash

   ```
   mkdir my-monorepo
   cd my-monorepo
   ```

2. Inside the `my-monorepo` directory, create two subdirectories: `shared` (for shared types) and `app` (for the main application):

   bash

   ```
   mkdir shared app
   ```

3. In the `shared` directory, create a `tsconfig.json` that defines the types for shared code:

json

```json
{
  "compilerOptions": {
    "composite": true,
    "declaration": true,
    "outDir": "../dist/shared",
    "baseUrl": "./"
  },
  "include": ["src/**/*"]
}
```

4. In the `app` directory, create another `tsconfig.json` to reference the `shared` project:

json

```json
{
  "compilerOptions": {
    "baseUrl": ".",
    "paths": {
      "@shared/*": ["../shared/src/*"]
    }
  },
  "references": [
    {
      "path": "../shared"
    }
  ],
  "include": ["src/**/*"]
}
```

- The `shared` project is marked as a composite project, which means it's designed to be referenced by other projects.
- The `app` project references the `shared` project and uses a **path alias** (`@shared/*`) to refer to the shared code.

11.2.1.2 Using Project References

Now you can reference the shared types in the `app` project like this:

```typescript
import { User } from '@shared/types';

const user: User = { id: 1, name: 'Alice' };
```

With project references in place:

- TypeScript understands the dependencies between `app` and `shared`.
- The `tsc` command will build the `shared` package first, then build the `app` package, ensuring that all references are properly resolved.

11.2.2 Path Aliases in TypeScript

Path aliases simplify the process of importing files across your project. Instead of using long relative paths like `../../../utils`, you can create a **path alias** that makes imports cleaner and more maintainable.

Here's how to set up path aliases in the `tsconfig.json` file:

```json
{
  "compilerOptions": {
    "baseUrl": ".",
    "paths": {
      "@utils/*": ["src/utils/*"]
    }
  }
}
```

Now, you can import files using the alias:

```typescript
import { helperFunction } from '@utils/helper';
```

This reduces the need for deep relative imports and improves readability, especially as your project structure becomes more complex.

11.3 Monorepo Setups with Yarn Workspaces or pnpm

A **monorepo** is a project structure where multiple packages or applications are stored in a single Git repository. Using a monorepo setup can help simplify dependency management, streamline collaboration, and maintain shared configurations across multiple packages.

There are several tools available to manage monorepos, such as **Yarn Workspaces** and **pnpm**. Both tools enable you to manage multiple packages in a single repository and handle dependencies efficiently.

11.3.1 Yarn Workspaces

Yarn Workspaces is a tool that simplifies dependency management in monorepos. It allows you to create multiple packages in a single repository while ensuring that shared dependencies are installed only once.

11.3.1.1 Setting Up Yarn Workspaces

1. Initialize a new project with Yarn:

```bash
yarn init -y
```

2. Add the following to your `package.json` to enable Yarn Workspaces:

```json
{
  "private": true,
  "workspaces": [
    "packages/*"
  ]
}
```

3. Create a `packages` directory and add two subdirectories: `app` and `shared`.

4. Inside `packages/app/package.json`, specify the dependencies for the application:

```json
{
  "name": "app",
  "version": "1.0.0",
  "dependencies": {
    "shared": "1.0.0"
  }
}
```

5. Inside `packages/shared/package.json`, specify the shared utilities or types:

```json
{
  "name": "shared",
  "version": "1.0.0"
}
```

6. Run `yarn install` to install all dependencies and link the `app` package to the `shared` package.

11.3.1.2 Benefits of Yarn Workspaces

- **Centralized Dependency Management**: Shared dependencies are installed once at the root level, reducing duplication.
- **Easier Versioning**: You can version and publish multiple related packages from a single repository.
- **Simplified Development Workflow**: Packages within the monorepo can reference each other using relative paths or package names, making it easy to work across different parts of the project.

11.3.2 pnpm

pnpm is another tool for managing monorepos. It is similar to Yarn Workspaces but uses a more efficient storage system to save disk space and improve installation speed.

11.3.2.1 Setting Up pnpm

1. Install pnpm globally:

   bash

   ```
   npm install -g pnpm
   ```

2. Initialize a new project with pnpm:

   bash

   ```
   pnpm init
   ```

3. Enable workspaces by adding the following to `pnpm-workspace.yaml`:

   yaml

```
packages:
  - "packages/*"
```

4. Create your `packages/app` and `packages/shared`
   directories, similar to the Yarn example.

11.3.2.2 Benefits of pnpm

- **Efficient Disk Usage**: pnpm uses hard links to save space
  by storing a single of each version of a package, reducing
  disk usage.
- **Faster Installations**: pnpm installs dependencies faster
  due to its efficient caching and deduplication mechanism.

11.4 Sharing Types and Utilities Across Packages

One of the main reasons for using a **monorepo** is to share code
between different packages. This can include **types**, **utilities**,
components, and other reusable modules.

11.4.1 Sharing Types Between Packages

In a monorepo setup, you can create a shared package for types
or utilities that can be consumed by other packages. For instance,
the `shared` package might contain common **DTOs** (Data Transfer
Objects), **interfaces**, and **types**.

11.4.1.1 Example of Shared Types

Let's say you have a `UserDto` in the `shared` package:

typescript

```
// packages/shared/src/types/UserDto.ts
export interface UserDto {
```

```
  id: number;
  name: string;
  email: string;
}
```

Now, in the `app` package, you can import and use the shared
`UserDto`:

typescript

```typescript
// packages/app/src/UserService.ts
import { UserDto } from 'shared/src/types/UserDto';

export const getUser = (id: number): UserDto => {
  // Logic to fetch user
  return { id, name: 'John Doe', email:
'john.doe@example.com' };
};
```

By sharing types between packages, you ensure **type
consistency** across your entire monorepo.

11.4.2 Sharing Utility Functions Between Packages

You can also share utility functions across packages in a similar
way. For example, the `shared` package might contain helper
functions like `formatDate`:

typescript

```typescript
// packages/shared/src/utils/formatDate.ts
export const formatDate = (date: Date): string => {
  return `${date.getFullYear()}-${date.getMonth() +
1}-${date.getDate()}`;
};
```

Now, you can import and use `formatDate` in the `app` package:

typescript

```ts
// packages/app/src/DateService.ts
import { formatDate } from
'shared/src/utils/formatDate';

export const displayDate = (date: Date): string => {
  return `The date is: ${formatDate(date)}`;
};
```

This allows you to centralize utility functions and types, making them easy to reuse across your entire monorepo.

11.5 Hands-On: Setting Up a Two-Package Monorepo

In this hands-on section, we'll set up a **two-package monorepo**: one for **shared types** and the other for the **main application**. We'll link them seamlessly and ensure they work together smoothly.

11.5.1 Initialize the Project

1. Create the root directory and initialize the monorepo:

    bash

    ```bash
    mkdir two-package-monorepo
    cd two-package-monorepo
    npm init -y
    ```

2. Create the `packages` directory:

    bash

    ```bash
    mkdir packages
    ```

3. Set up the root `package.json` to enable Yarn Workspaces or pnpm:

```json
{
  "private": true,
  "workspaces": ["packages/*"]
}
```

11.5.2 Create the Shared Package

1. Inside the `packages` directory, create a `shared` package:

```bash
mkdir packages/shared
cd packages/shared
npm init -y
```

2. Create a `UserDto.ts` file for shared types:

```typescript
// packages/shared/src/types/UserDto.ts
export interface UserDto {
  id: number;
  name: string;
  email: string;
}
```

3. Add `tsconfig.json` for the shared package:

```json
{
  "compilerOptions": {
    "composite": true,
    "declaration": true,
    "outDir": "../../dist/shared",
    "baseUrl": "./"
  },
  "include": ["src/**/*"]
}
```

11.5.3 Create the App Package

1. Inside `packages`, create the `app` package:

    bash

    ```bash
    mkdir packages/app
    cd packages/app
    npm init -y
    ```

2. Add `tsconfig.json` for the app package:

    json

    ```json
    {
      "compilerOptions": {
        "baseUrl": ".",
        "paths": {
          "@shared/*": ["../shared/src/*"]
        }
      },
      "references": [
        {
          "path": "../shared"
        }
      ],
      "include": ["src/**/*"]
    }
    ```

3. Create a simple app service that uses the shared types:

    typescript

    ```typescript
    // packages/app/src/UserService.ts
    import { UserDto } from
    '@shared/types/UserDto';

    export const getUser = (id: number): UserDto =>
    {
      return { id, name: "Alice", email:
    "alice@example.com" };
    };
    ```

11.5.4 Link the Packages

1. Go back to the root of the project and run:

   ```bash
   yarn install  # Or pnpm install
   ```

2. The packages are now linked, and the shared types and utilities are accessible from the `app` package.

Conclusion

In this chapter, we've explored **organizing large-scale TypeScript projects** using techniques like **project references**, **path aliases**, and **composite projects**. We also looked into **monorepo setups** with **Yarn Workspaces** and **pnpm**, making it easier to manage multiple related packages in a single repository.

The **hands-on project** showed you how to set up a two-package monorepo: one for shared types and one for an application, linking them seamlessly.

With these tools and practices, you can maintain a scalable, clean, and type-safe codebase, even as your project grows in complexity.

Chapter 12: Packaging and Publishing Libraries

12.1 Introduction to Packaging and Publishing Libraries

When you create a reusable TypeScript library, it's essential to ensure that it can be easily consumed by other developers or applications. This involves:

1. **Bundling** the code for different module formats (like **ES modules (ESM)** and **CommonJS (CJS)**).
2. **Generating declaration files (.d.ts)** that describe the types in your library, ensuring type safety for consumers.
3. **Semantic versioning** to ensure that changes to the library are clearly communicated to its users.
4. **Automating the release process** using **CI/CD** (Continuous Integration/Continuous Delivery) pipelines.

By following these steps, you can publish a TypeScript-based library to **npm** and ensure that it is easy to maintain and upgrade over time. This chapter will cover the tools and techniques needed to achieve all of this, including **Rollup, webpack**, and **semantic versioning**.

12.2 Bundling with Rollup or Webpack for ES and CJS Outputs

Bundling is the process of taking all of your source code, along with any dependencies, and creating a **single file** (or multiple files) that can be used in different environments. **Rollup** and **webpack** are two popular bundlers used for this purpose.

12.2.1 Rollup for Bundling

Rollup is a JavaScript module bundler that is particularly well-suited for libraries, as it produces **smaller, optimized bundles** and supports **tree-shaking** (removing unused code). Rollup is an excellent choice for libraries that need to output **ES modules (ESM)**.

12.2.1.1 Setting Up Rollup

To use **Rollup** for bundling your library, follow these steps:

1. Install the necessary dependencies:

   ```bash
   npm install --save-dev rollup rollup-plugin-typescript2 typescript
   ```

2. Create a `rollup.config.js` configuration file:

   ```javascript
   import typescript from 'rollup-plugin-typescript2';
   import pkg from './package.json';

   export default {
     input: 'src/index.ts',  // Entry file
     output: [
       {
         file: pkg.main,  // CommonJS output
         format: 'cjs',
         sourcemap: true,
       },
       {
         file: pkg.module,  // ES module output
         format: 'esm',
         sourcemap: true,
       },
     ],
   ```

```
    plugins: [
      typescript({
        tsconfig: './tsconfig.json', // Path to
tsconfig.json
      }),
    ],
    external: Object.keys(pkg.dependencies ||
{}),
  };
```

- o **input**: Specifies the entry file for your library
  (usually `src/index.ts`).
- o **output**: Defines the formats you want to bundle.
  Common formats include `cjs` (CommonJS) and
  `esm` (ES modules).
- o **external**: Excludes dependencies from the bundle
  (useful for external dependencies like `react` or
  `lodash`).

3. Add the **output paths** to your `package.json`:

json

```json
{
  "main": "dist/my-library.cjs.js",
  "module": "dist/my-library.esm.js",
  "types": "dist/index.d.ts",
  "scripts": {
    "build": "rollup -c"
  }
}
```

- o The **main** field points to the **CommonJS** output file,
  while the **module** field points to the **ES module**
  output.
- o **types** points to the generated `.d.ts` declaration
  file.

4. Run the Rollup build process:

bash

```bash
npm run build
```

Rollup will bundle your TypeScript code and create both **CommonJS** and **ES module** outputs, ready to be published.

12.2.2 Webpack for Bundling

webpack is another bundler, but it's more commonly used for **applications** rather than libraries. However, it can still be used for bundling libraries, especially if you need more advanced features like **code splitting** or **asset management**.

12.2.2.1 Setting Up Webpack

To use **webpack** for bundling your TypeScript library, follow these steps:

1. Install the necessary dependencies:

    bash

    ```bash
    npm install --save-dev webpack webpack-cli ts-loader typescript
    ```

2. Create a `webpack.config.js` configuration file:

    javascript

    ```javascript
    const path = require('path');

    module.exports = {
      entry: './src/index.ts',
      output: {
        filename: 'my-library.bundle.js',
        path: path.resolve(__dirname, 'dist'),
        library: 'MyLibrary',
        libraryTarget: 'umd',  // Universal Module
    Definition (CJS/AMD/ESM)
      },
      resolve: {
        extensions: ['.ts', '.js'],
      },
      module: {
    ```

```
    rules: [
      {
        test: /\.ts$/,
        use: 'ts-loader',
        exclude: /node_modules/,
      },
    ],
  },
};
```

3. Add build scripts to `package.json`:

```json
{
  "scripts": {
    "build": "webpack"
  }
}
```

4. Run the webpack build process:

```bash
npm run build
```

With this setup, webpack will bundle your library into a **UMD** (Universal Module Definition) format, making it compatible with **CommonJS**, **AMD**, and **ES modules**.

12.3 Generating and Distributing `.d.ts` Declaration Files

TypeScript uses **declaration files** (`.d.ts`) to define the types for your library. These files are critical when you're distributing your TypeScript library, as they allow consumers of the library to have full type support when using it.

12.3.1 Generating Declaration Files

To ensure that TypeScript users get type definitions for your library, you need to generate **declaration files** during the build process. This is done by setting `declaration: true` in your `tsconfig.json` file.

1. In your `tsconfig.json`, ensure that the **declaration** and **outDir** are set:

   json

   ```json
   {
     "compilerOptions": {
       "declaration": true,
       "outDir": "./dist",
       "rootDir": "./src",
       "strict": true,
       "moduleResolution": "node",
       "esModuleInterop": true
     }
   }
   ```

   - **declaration** tells TypeScript to generate `.d.ts` files alongside the compiled JavaScript.
   - **outDir** specifies where the `.d.ts` files and the compiled JavaScript files will be output.

2. After running the build, TypeScript will generate `.d.ts` files in the output directory (`dist/`).

12.3.2 Distributing the `.d.ts` Files

Once the `.d.ts` files are generated, ensure they are included in your **npm package**. In your `package.json`, ensure that the **types** field points to the generated `.d.ts` file:

json

```json
{
  "types": "dist/index.d.ts"
```

```
}
```

When users install your library via npm, TypeScript will automatically use the generated declaration files to provide **type checking** and **intellisense** for your library.

12.4 Semantic Versioning and Changelog Automation

Proper versioning is essential for maintaining backward compatibility and clear communication with library consumers. **Semantic Versioning (SemVer)** is the standard for versioning libraries, and it's based on the following format:

```
MAJOR.MINOR.PATCH
```

- **MAJOR** version changes when you make incompatible API changes.
- **MINOR** version changes when you add functionality in a backward-compatible manner.
- **PATCH** version changes when you make backward-compatible fixes or improvements.

12.4.1 Managing Versions with `npm version`

You can use the `npm version` command to automatically update your library's version based on changes to the code.

For example:

```bash
npm version patch   # Increments the PATCH version
npm version minor   # Increments the MINOR version
npm version major   # Increments the MAJOR version
```

This will update the version in your `package.json` and create a **git tag** for the version.

12.4.2 Automating the Changelog with `standard-version`

Automating the generation of changelogs can save a lot of time and ensure consistency. **standard-version** is a tool that automates **semantic versioning** and changelog generation based on commit messages.

1. Install `standard-version`:

   ```bash
   npm install --save-dev standard-version
   ```

2. Add a release script in your `package.json`:

   ```json
   {
     "scripts": {
       "release": "standard-version"
     }
   }
   ```

3. When you run `npm run release`, **standard-version** will:
   - Automatically bump the version based on the commits.
   - Generate a changelog that summarizes the changes since the last release.

12.5 Hands-On: Publish a Small Utility Library to npm

In this section, we'll walk through the process of publishing a small utility library to **npm**, complete with **CI-driven release steps**.

12.5.1 Initialize the Project

1. Create a new directory for your utility library:

   bash

   ```bash
   mkdir my-utils
   cd my-utils
   npm init -y
   ```

2. Set up **TypeScript**:

   bash

   ```bash
   npm install --save-dev typescript
   ```

3. Create the `tsconfig.json` file:

   json

   ```json
   {
     "compilerOptions": {
       "declaration": true,
       "outDir": "./dist",
       "rootDir": "./src",
       "strict": true,
       "moduleResolution": "node"
     },
     "include": ["src/**/*"]
   }
   ```

12.5.2 Writing the Utility Function

Create a small utility function in the `src` directory, for example, a function that formats dates:

typescript

```typescript
// src/formatDate.ts
export const formatDate = (date: Date): string => {
  return `${date.getFullYear()}-${date.getMonth() +
1}-${date.getDate()}`;
```

```
};
```

12.5.3 Bundling the Library

Set up **Rollup** (as described earlier) to bundle the utility library
into CommonJS and ES modules.

```bash
bash
```

```bash
npm install --save-dev rollup rollup-plugin-
typescript2
```

Configure `rollup.config.js` to generate both **ESM** and **CJS**
outputs.

12.5.4 Publishing to npm

1. Make sure you are logged into your **npm** account:

   ```bash
   bash
   ```

   ```bash
   npm login
   ```

2. Publish your library:

   ```bash
   bash
   ```

   ```bash
   npm publish --access public
   ```

12.5.5 Automating Releases with GitHub Actions

To automate the release process, use **GitHub Actions** for CI/CD.
Create a `.github/workflows/release.yml` file:

```yaml
yaml
```

```yaml
name: Release

on:
  push:
    branches:
```

```
      - main
    tags:
      - 'v*'

jobs:
  release:
    runs-on: ubuntu-latest
    steps:
      - name: Checkout code
        uses: actions/checkout@v2
      - name: Set up Node.js
        uses: actions/setup-node@v2
        with:
          node-version: '14'
      - name: Install dependencies
        run: npm install
      - name: Run tests
        run: npm test
      - name: Create release
        run: npm run release
```

This workflow will:

- Automatically trigger on every push to the `main` branch.
- Run tests and generate a new release using `standard-version`.

Conclusion

In this chapter, we've covered how to **package** and **publish libraries** with TypeScript, ensuring they are maintainable, versioned properly, and ready for distribution. You learned how to:

1. Bundle your library for both **ES** and **CJS** formats using **Rollup**.
2. Generate and distribute **TypeScript declaration files** to provide type safety.
3. Use **semantic versioning** and automate changelog generation with **standard-version**.

4. **Hands-on**: Publish a utility library to **npm**, automating releases with **GitHub Actions**.

By following these steps, you can efficiently develop, maintain, and distribute **TypeScript libraries**, making them reusable and easy for others to integrate into their projects.

Chapter 13: Optimizing Bundle Size and Performance

13.1 Introduction to Bundle Size and Performance

When building modern web applications, one of the key factors in improving user experience is ensuring that your app loads quickly. The **bundle size** is a crucial part of this, as large JavaScript bundles can lead to **slower load times**, especially on slower networks or devices. Optimizing bundle size directly impacts the speed and responsiveness of your application.

By applying performance optimization techniques like **tree shaking**, **code splitting**, and **lazy loading**, you can minimize the amount of JavaScript code the browser needs to download, parse, and execute. This helps your app load faster and feel more responsive.

In this chapter, we will explore the following key topics:

1. **Tree shaking, code splitting**, and **lazy loading**.
2. Analyzing bundle contents using **source-map explorer**.
3. Fine-tuning **Webpack** and **Rollup** settings for optimal performance.
4. **Hands-on**: Profiling a demo app's bundle size and applying **dynamic imports** to reduce the initial load.

13.2 Tree Shaking, Code Splitting, and Lazy Loading

13.2.1 Tree Shaking

Tree shaking is a process where unused code is removed from the final bundle. This technique relies on **ES modules** (ESM) and is most effective when using bundlers like **Webpack** or **Rollup** that support tree shaking.

In order for tree shaking to work, your code must follow the **ES module** syntax. This means using `import` and `export` statements, rather than `require()` or `module.exports`.

13.2.1.1 How Tree Shaking Works

Tree shaking works by analyzing the **dependency graph** of your application and determining which parts of the code are not used anywhere. These unused parts are then removed from the final bundle, resulting in smaller file sizes.

Here's an example:

typescript

```
// utils.ts
export const add = (a: number, b: number) => a + b;
export const multiply = (a: number, b: number) => a *
b;

// app.ts
import { add } from './utils';

console.log(add(2, 3));
```

- In this example, the `multiply` function is not used in `app.ts`.
- **Tree shaking** will remove the unused `multiply` function from the final bundle, reducing its size.

13.2.1.2 Enabling Tree Shaking in Webpack and Rollup

For **Webpack**, tree shaking is enabled by default when you use **ES modules** and set the `mode` to `production`:

```javascript
module.exports = {
  mode: 'production',
  // other configurations
};
```

For **Rollup**, tree shaking is also enabled by default. You just need to make sure you're using the `esm` format and not `cjs` (CommonJS), as `cjs` doesn't support tree shaking.

```javascript
export default {
  input: 'src/index.ts',
  output: {
    file: 'dist/bundle.js',
    format: 'esm',  // Ensures tree shaking works
  },
  plugins: [typescript()],
};
```

13.2.2 Code Splitting

Code splitting is a technique that allows you to split your application's bundle into smaller chunks that can be loaded on demand. This helps reduce the initial load time of your app, as only the required code is loaded initially, and the rest is loaded as needed.

There are several ways to implement code splitting, including **manual splitting** and **dynamic imports**.

13.2.2.1 Manual Code Splitting

In **Webpack**, you can manually define entry points that will be split into separate bundles:

```javascript
```

```
module.exports = {
  entry: {
    main: './src/index.js',
    vendor: './src/vendor.js',
  },
  output: {
    filename: '[name].bundle.js',
    path: path.resolve(__dirname, 'dist'),
  },
};
```

In this example, `main.bundle.js` and `vendor.bundle.js` will be generated separately. The browser can then load the necessary bundle only when needed.

13.2.2.2 Dynamic Imports (Lazy Loading)

The more modern approach to code splitting is **lazy loading** using **dynamic imports**. This allows you to split your code into smaller chunks that are loaded only when needed.

For example, in a React application:

typescript

```typescript
import React, { Suspense } from 'react';

// Dynamically import the component only when needed
const LazyComponent = React.lazy(() =>
import('./LazyComponent'));

const App = () => (
  <div>
    <Suspense fallback={<div>Loading...</div>}>
      <LazyComponent />
    </Suspense>
  </div>
);
```

- The `LazyComponent` will only be loaded when it's rendered, not at the initial load.
- The browser will download the chunk only when required, reducing the initial bundle size.

13.2.3 Lazy Loading Images and Assets

In addition to lazy loading JavaScript, you can also **lazy load images** and other assets to reduce the initial load time. This can be done using the `loading="lazy"` attribute for images:

html

```html
<img src="image.jpg" loading="lazy" alt="Example" />
```

This will instruct the browser to load the image only when it's about to be displayed in the viewport, thus saving bandwidth and improving load times.

13.3 Analyzing Bundle Contents with Source Map Explorer

After applying tree shaking and code splitting, it's important to analyze the contents of your bundles to identify any unnecessary or oversized files that could be affecting performance.

13.3.1 Setting Up Source Map Explorer

source-map-explorer is a tool that helps you visualize the contents of your JavaScript bundle and see what's contributing to its size. It uses the **source maps** generated during bundling to provide a clear, graphical representation of your bundle.

13.3.1.1 Installing Source Map Explorer

1. Install `source-map-explorer`:

```bash
bash

npm install --save-dev source-map-explorer
```

2. In your `package.json`, add a script to run the tool:

```json
json

{
  "scripts": {
    "analyze": "source-map-explorer
'dist/*.js'"
  }
}
```

13.3.1.2 Analyzing the Bundle

After bundling your application, run the following command to visualize the contents:

```bash
bash

npm run analyze
```

This will open a graphical representation of your bundle, showing the sizes of individual modules and helping you identify large dependencies that might be optimized further.

13.3.2 Interpreting the Results

The **source-map-explorer** visualization will show you the following:

- **Large libraries**: Identify any large dependencies (like React or Lodash) that contribute significantly to the bundle size.
- **Unwanted dependencies**: See if any unused or unnecessary dependencies are included in the bundle.
- **Redundant code**: Spot any duplicate code that could be eliminated with proper tree shaking or code splitting.

This analysis helps you make informed decisions about which parts of the code or dependencies to optimize.

13.4 Fine-Tuning Webpack/Rollup Settings

13.4.1 Optimizing Webpack

Webpack is a powerful bundler, but its configurations can become complex. To optimize Webpack, you can fine-tune various settings to reduce bundle size and improve performance.

13.4.1.1 Using `TerserPlugin` for Minification

Webpack uses **TerserPlugin** for minifying JavaScript code. This can be enabled in the `optimization` section of your Webpack configuration:

javascript

```javascript
module.exports = {
  mode: 'production',
  optimization: {
    minimize: true,
    minimizer: [new TerserPlugin()],
  },
};
```

This will minify the JavaScript output, removing whitespace, comments, and unnecessary code, which significantly reduces the bundle size.

13.4.1.2 Enabling Cache for Faster Builds

Webpack allows you to cache modules to speed up subsequent builds. To enable caching, use the following configuration:

javascript

```
module.exports = {
  cache: {
    type: 'filesystem',
  },
};
```

This caches the build artifacts on the filesystem, so that Webpack only rebuilds the parts of the project that have changed, improving build times.

13.4.2 Optimizing Rollup

Rollup is another popular bundler, particularly for libraries. While Rollup is optimized for smaller bundles by default, you can still fine-tune its performance using plugins.

13.4.2.1 Using `rollup-plugin-terser` for Minification

Rollup also supports **code minification** using the `rollup-plugin-terser` plugin:

```bash
npm install --save-dev rollup-plugin-terser
```

Then, update your `rollup.config.js`:

```javascript
import { terser } from 'rollup-plugin-terser';

export default {
  input: 'src/index.ts',
  output: {
    file: 'dist/bundle.min.js',
    format: 'esm',
  },
  plugins: [terser()],
};
```

This will minify the output and reduce the file size.

13.4.2.2 Tree Shaking and External Dependencies

Rollup works best with **ES modules**, and it supports tree shaking out of the box. To exclude certain dependencies from your bundle and treat them as external, you can specify them in the `external` option:

```javascript
export default {
  input: 'src/index.ts',
  output: {
    file: 'dist/bundle.js',
    format: 'esm',
  },
  external: ['react', 'lodash'],
};
```

This ensures that **React** and **Lodash** are not included in the bundle, reducing the size, and allowing them to be loaded externally.

13.5 Hands-On: Profiling a Demo App's Bundle Size

In this hands-on section, we will profile a simple **React app** and optimize its bundle size using **dynamic imports** to reduce the initial load.

13.5.1 Setting Up the Demo App

1. Initialize a new **React app**:

   ```bash
   ```

```
npx create-react-app bundle-optimization-demo -
-template typescript
cd bundle-optimization-demo
```

2. Install **source-map-explorer** for bundle analysis:

```bash
npm install --save-dev source-map-explorer
```

3. Build the app for production:

```bash
npm run build
```

13.5.2 Analyzing the Bundle

Run **source-map-explorer** to visualize the bundle:

```bash
npx source-map-explorer 'build/static/js/*.js'
```

This will open a visualization of your app's bundle, helping identify large dependencies like React or other libraries.

13.5.3 Applying Dynamic Imports to Reduce Initial Load

Next, let's apply **dynamic imports** to split the bundle and reduce the initial load.

```tsx
import React, { Suspense } from 'react';

// Lazy load the component
const LazyComponent = React.lazy(() =>
import('./LazyComponent'));

const App: React.FC = () => (
```

```
<div>
  <Suspense fallback={<div>Loading...</div>}>
    <LazyComponent />
  </Suspense>
</div>
);

export default App;
```

In this example:

- The LazyComponent is only loaded when needed, reducing the size of the initial bundle.
- **Suspense** is used to handle the loading state while the component is being fetched.

13.5.4 Rebuilding and Analyzing Again

After applying dynamic imports, rebuild the app and analyze the bundle again to confirm the reduction in size.

```bash
npm run build
npx source-map-explorer 'build/static/js/*.js'
```

Conclusion

In this chapter, we covered various techniques to **optimize bundle size** and improve the performance of TypeScript-based web applications. We explored:

- **Tree shaking** to remove unused code and reduce bundle size.
- **Code splitting** and **lazy loading** to split the application into smaller, on-demand chunks.
- Analyzing bundles with **source-map-explorer** to understand the contents and identify opportunities for optimization.

- Fine-tuning bundlers like **Webpack** and **Rollup** for improved performance.

The **hands-on section** showed how to profile a **React app's bundle size**, and apply **dynamic imports** to reduce the initial load.

By following these strategies, you can optimize the performance of your TypeScript-based applications, improving both the user experience and overall efficiency of your web app.

Chapter 14: Designing Scalable Microservices

14.1 Introduction to Microservices Architecture

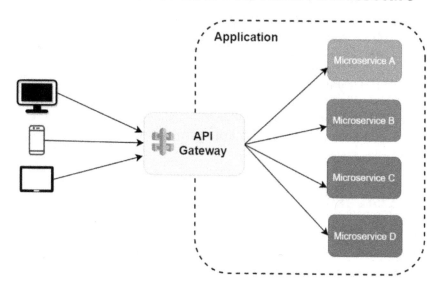

Microservices architecture is a design pattern in which an application is broken down into smaller, **independent services** that can be developed, deployed, and maintained separately. This approach contrasts with the **monolithic architecture**, where the entire application is tightly coupled in one codebase.

In a microservices-based system, each service:

- Handles a specific business function.
- Communicates with other services through well-defined interfaces (typically via **APIs** or **message queues**).
- Can be developed and deployed independently.

TypeScript is an ideal language for building microservices, as it ensures **type safety** across all services, providing clarity and consistency in the data exchanged between services.

In this chapter, we will:

1. Break a system into **typed services**, ensuring strong type safety across your microservices.
2. Discuss different communication mechanisms for microservices: **REST**, **gRPC**, and **message queues**.
3. Containerize services using **Docker** and orchestrate them with **Kubernetes** to ensure scalability and easy deployment.
4. **Hands-on**: Containerize a sample **TypeScript microservice**, deploy it locally using **Docker Compose**, and test **inter-service communication**.

14.2 Breaking a System into Typed Services

The core idea of **microservices** is to break down a large system into smaller, **self-contained services** that focus on specific tasks. Each service can communicate with other services via standardized APIs or messaging systems.

14.2.1 Defining Typed Services

In a **typed** microservice system, it's essential to ensure that each service exposes well-defined interfaces. These interfaces could be RESTful APIs, gRPC endpoints, or even messages in a queue. TypeScript helps here by ensuring that the data flowing between services adheres to a specified contract.

For example, in a **user service**, you might define the following TypeScript interfaces:

typescript

```
// user.types.ts
export interface CreateUserDto {
  name: string;
  email: string;
}

export interface User {
  id: string;
  name: string;
  email: string;
}
```

- **CreateUserDto** is the type for the payload used to create a new user.
- **User** is the type for the user data that is returned or stored in the system.

With this **typed contract**, other services consuming the **user service** can expect the same structure, improving **type safety** across the entire system.

14.2.2 Service Boundaries and Domain-Driven Design (DDD)

When breaking down a system into microservices, **Domain-Driven Design (DDD)** can be a helpful approach. DDD focuses on organizing services around the **business domain** rather than technical concerns. Each microservice should encapsulate a specific domain and handle its business logic.

For example, in an e-commerce platform:

- A **user service** might handle authentication, registration, and profile management.
- An **order service** could handle the creation, tracking, and management of orders.
- A **product service** would manage product catalogs, pricing, and availability.

These boundaries help to create clear, independent services that can evolve separately.

14.3 Communicating Between Microservices

The next challenge in designing microservices is ensuring that these independent services can **communicate** with each other. The main communication methods are:

1. **REST APIs**: A traditional, stateless communication mechanism using HTTP.
2. **gRPC**: A high-performance, language-agnostic remote procedure call (RPC) framework that uses Protocol Buffers for serializing data.
3. **Message Queues**: Asynchronous communication using queues to decouple services and allow for more flexible workflows.

14.3.1 RESTful APIs

REST (Representational State Transfer) is a widely used communication mechanism in microservices. Services expose **endpoints** that can be consumed by other services over HTTP. RESTful APIs are simple to implement and are compatible with most web technologies.

Here's an example of a RESTful API in **Express** that provides access to user data:

```typescript
import express, { Request, Response } from 'express';
import { User, CreateUserDto } from './user.types';

const app = express();
app.use(express.json());

const users: User[] = [];
```

```
// POST /users - Create a new user
app.post('/users', (req: Request, res: Response) => {
  const userData: CreateUserDto = req.body;
  const newUser: User = { id: Date.now().toString(),
...userData };
  users.push(newUser);
  res.status(201).json(newUser);
});

// GET /users - Get all users
app.get('/users', (req: Request, res: Response) => {
  res.json(users);
});

app.listen(3000, () => {
  console.log('User service is running on
http://localhost:3000');
});
```

In this example:

- The **user service** exposes two REST endpoints: POST
  /users to create users and GET /users to fetch all users.
- Other microservices can consume these APIs over HTTP,
  ensuring clear communication via **typed** payloads.

14.3.2 gRPC for High-Performance Communication

gRPC is a powerful alternative to REST, providing **faster** and
more efficient communication between microservices. It uses
Protocol Buffers (a binary format) for serializing data, which
reduces the payload size compared to JSON.

To use **gRPC** in TypeScript, you need to define a **Proto file** that
specifies the service methods and data types. For example:

```
proto

// user.proto
syntax = "proto3";
```

```
service UserService {
  rpc CreateUser (CreateUserRequest) returns
(UserResponse);
}

message CreateUserRequest {
  string name = 1;
  string email = 2;
}

message UserResponse {
  string id = 1;
  string name = 2;
  string email = 3;
}
```

- **Proto files** define the gRPC service methods (e.g., `CreateUser`) and message formats (`CreateUserRequest` and `UserResponse`).

Once the **Proto file** is defined, you can generate TypeScript code using tools like `grpc-tools` or `@grpc/proto-loader` to interact with the service.

14.3.3 Message Queues for Asynchronous Communication

In some cases, microservices need to communicate asynchronously. **Message queues** allow services to send messages to a queue, which are processed by other services at a later time. This is useful for decoupling services and allowing them to work independently.

Commonly used message queue systems include:

- **RabbitMQ**
- **Apache Kafka**
- **Amazon SQS**

Here's an example of sending and receiving a message with **RabbitMQ** in Node.js:

```typescript
import amqp from 'amqplib';

async function sendMessage(message: string) {
  const connection = await
amqp.connect('amqp://localhost');
  const channel = await connection.createChannel();
  const queue = 'userQueue';

  await channel.assertQueue(queue, { durable: true
});
  channel.sendToQueue(queue, Buffer.from(message), {
persistent: true });

  console.log(" [x] Sent %s", message);
}

sendMessage('New user created');
```

- Services can send messages to a queue, which can be processed by other microservices. This provides **asynchronous communication**, allowing services to be more flexible and resilient.

14.4 Containerizing Services with Docker and Orchestrating with Kubernetes

One of the key advantages of microservices is the ability to **deploy each service independently**. Using **Docker** for containerization and **Kubernetes** for orchestration, you can scale your services easily and ensure they run consistently across different environments.

14.4.1 Docker for Containerizing Microservices

Docker allows you to package your microservices in lightweight, portable containers. These containers can run on any system that supports Docker, ensuring that your application works the same in development, staging, and production environments.

14.4.1.1 Dockerizing a TypeScript Microservice

1. Create a `Dockerfile` for the TypeScript-based microservice:

   ```
   Dockerfile

   # Use official Node.js image as base image
   FROM node:16

   # Set working directory
   WORKDIR /app

   #  package.json and package-lock.json
    package*.json ./

   # Install dependencies
   RUN npm install

   #  the rest of the application code
    . .

   # Build the TypeScript code
   RUN npm run build

   # Expose port 3000
   EXPOSE 3000

   # Start the application
   CMD ["npm", "start"]
   ```

2. Build and run the Docker container:

   ```bash
   bash
   ```

```
docker build -t user-service .
docker run -p 3000:3000 user-service
```

This will run the **user service** inside a Docker container, making it easy to deploy and manage in various environments.

14.4.2 Orchestrating with Kubernetes

While Docker helps you containerize services, **Kubernetes** allows you to orchestrate and manage the deployment, scaling, and monitoring of these containers.

To deploy a TypeScript microservice with **Kubernetes**, you need to define a **Kubernetes deployment** and **service** YAML file:

yaml

```yaml
# user-service-deployment.yaml
apiVersion: apps/v1
kind: Deployment
metadata:
  name: user-service
spec:
  replicas: 3
  selector:
    matchLabels:
      app: user-service
  template:
    metadata:
      labels:
        app: user-service
    spec:
      containers:
        - name: user-service
          image: user-service:latest
          ports:
            - containerPort: 3000
---
apiVersion: v1
kind: Service
metadata:
```

```
    name: user-service
spec:
  selector:
    app: user-service
  ports:
    - protocol: TCP
      port: 80
      targetPort: 3000
  type: LoadBalancer
```

- The **deployment** defines how many instances of the service should run, and the **service** exposes the microservice to external traffic.

To deploy the service to Kubernetes, use the following command:

bash

```
kubectl apply -f user-service-deployment.yaml
```

Kubernetes will manage the deployment, scaling, and health of the service, ensuring high availability and easy management.

14.5 Hands-On: Containerize a TypeScript Microservice and Test Inter-Service Calls

In this hands-on section, we will containerize a simple **TypeScript microservice**, deploy it locally with **Docker Compose**, and test the inter-service communication between two services.

14.5.1 Setting Up the Services

1. Create two microservices: **user-service** and **order-service**. Both services will be simple **Express** apps built with **TypeScript**.
2. Define basic endpoints for both services. For example, the **user-service** will expose a GET /users endpoint, and the

order-service will expose a `POST` `/orders` endpoint that references a user.

14.5.2 Create Dockerfiles for Both Services

1. **User Service Dockerfile:**

```
Dockerfile

FROM node:16
WORKDIR /app
 package*.json ./
RUN npm install
 . .
RUN npm run build
EXPOSE 3000
CMD ["npm", "start"]
```

2. **Order Service Dockerfile:**

```
Dockerfile

FROM node:16
WORKDIR /app
 package*.json ./
RUN npm install
 . .
RUN npm run build
EXPOSE 3001
CMD ["npm", "start"]
```

14.5.3 Docker Compose for Local Deployment

1. Create a `docker-compose.yml` file to manage both services:

```yaml
version: '3'
services:
  user-service:
    build: ./user-service
```

```
    ports:
        - "3000:3000"
    order-service:
        build: ./order-service
        ports:
            - "3001:3001"
```

2. Run the services with **Docker Compose**:

```bash
bash

docker-compose up --build
```

14.5.4 Testing Inter-Service Communication

1. Test inter-service communication by having the **order-service** call the **user-service** to retrieve user data. You can use **Axios** to make HTTP requests between services.

```typescript
typescript

import axios from 'axios';

// In order-service
const createOrder = async (userId: string) => {
  const userResponse = await
axios.get(`http://user-
service:3000/users/${userId}`);
  const user = userResponse.data;
  console.log('Order created for user:',
user.name);
};
```

2. Test the communication by creating an order from the **order-service** and verifying that it successfully fetches user information from the **user-service**.

Conclusion

In this chapter, we explored how to design **scalable microservices** in TypeScript. We covered:

1. Breaking down a system into **typed services** and ensuring strong type safety using TypeScript interfaces.
2. Different communication methods between services, including **REST**, **gRPC**, and **message queues**.
3. **Containerizing** microservices with **Docker** and orchestrating them with **Kubernetes**.
4. **Hands-on**: Containerizing a TypeScript-based microservice, deploying it locally using **Docker Compose**, and testing inter-service communication.

By following these best practices, you can build **scalable, maintainable**, and **efficient microservices** that can be deployed and managed easily in modern environments

Chapter 15: Capstone: Full-Stack TypeScript Application

15.1 Introduction to Building Full-Stack Applications with TypeScript

Building a **full-stack application** involves connecting the **frontend** and **backend** to create a fully functional, interactive system. Using **TypeScript** throughout the entire stack offers several benefits:

- **Consistency**: By using the same language across the stack, you can ensure a unified development experience.
- **Type Safety**: TypeScript helps catch errors at compile-time, preventing many common runtime errors.
- **Maintainability**: Strong typing and clear interfaces make maintaining the application easier as the codebase grows.

In this chapter, we will cover the following topics:

1. Putting all pieces together: the **frontend**, **backend**, and **services**.
2. Setting up a **CI/CD pipeline** to automate builds and deployments.
3. Implementing **monitoring** and **logging** to ensure the application runs smoothly in production.
4. Best practices for maintaining and scaling the application over time.

15.2 Putting All Pieces Together: Frontend, Backend, and Services

A modern full-stack application consists of several layers:

1. **Frontend**: The client-side application, typically built using a framework like **React**, which handles user interactions and communicates with the backend.
2. **Backend**: The server-side application, typically built using a framework like **Express** in **Node.js**, which processes requests, interacts with databases, and exposes APIs.
3. **Microservices**: Independent services responsible for specific tasks (e.g., notifications, authentication) that communicate with the backend and/or each other via APIs or message queues.

In a **TypeScript-based** stack, both the frontend and backend share **type definitions** (via **interfaces** or **DTOs**) to ensure that the data exchanged between the two layers is consistent and type-safe.

15.2.1 Frontend with React

The frontend of the task management application will be built using **React**, a popular library for building user interfaces. TypeScript is used with React to ensure type safety in components, props, state, and events.

Setting Up the Frontend

1. First, create a new React app using TypeScript:

```bash
npx create-react-app task-manager-frontend --template typescript
cd task-manager-frontend
```

2. Install **Axios** for making HTTP requests:

```bash
npm install axios
```

3. Create a simple **task list component** in `src/components/TaskList.tsx`:

```tsx
import React, { useState, useEffect } from 'react';
import axios from 'axios';

interface Task {
  id: string;
  name: string;
  completed: boolean;
}

const TaskList: React.FC = () => {
  const [tasks, setTasks] =
useState<Task[]>([]);

  useEffect(() => {
    axios.get('http://localhost:5000/tasks')
      .then(response => {
        setTasks(response.data);
      })
      .catch(error => console.error('Error
fetching tasks', error));
  }, []);

  return (
    <div>
      <h1>Task List</h1>
      <ul>
        {tasks.map(task => (
          <li key={task.id}>
            {task.name} - {task.completed ?
'Completed' : 'Pending'}
          </li>
```

```
        ))}
      </ul>
    </div>
  );
};

export default TaskList;
```

- This component fetches a list of tasks from the **Express backend** and displays them.
- The `Task` interface defines the shape of the task object, ensuring type safety in the component.

15.2.2 Backend with Express

The backend will be built using **Express**, a minimalist web framework for **Node.js**. The backend handles business logic, stores data, and exposes APIs that the frontend can interact with.

Setting Up the Backend

1. Initialize the **Express API**:

   bash

   ```bash
   mkdir task-manager-backend
   cd task-manager-backend
   npm init -y
   npm install express axios
   npm install --save-dev typescript
   @types/express @types/node
   ```

2. Create a `tsconfig.json` file to enable TypeScript support:

   json

   ```json
   {
     "compilerOptions": {
       "target": "ES6",
       "module": "commonjs",
       "declaration": true,
   ```

```
    "outDir": "./dist",
    "rootDir": "./src",
    "strict": true,
    "esModuleInterop": true,
    "skipLibCheck": true
  },
  "include": ["src/**/*.ts"]
}
```

3. **Create the main Express server in** `src/server.ts`:

typescript

```typescript
import express, { Request, Response } from
'express';

const app = express();
const port = 5000;

interface Task {
  id: string;
  name: string;
  completed: boolean;
}

let tasks: Task[] = [
  { id: '1', name: 'Do the laundry', completed:
false },
  { id: '2', name: 'Write TypeScript code',
completed: false },
];

app.get('/tasks', (req: Request, res: Response)
=> {
  res.json(tasks);
});

app.listen(port, () => {
  console.log(`Server running on
http://localhost:${port}`);
});
```

- This backend serves a list of tasks at the `/tasks` endpoint, which the frontend will consume.

15.2.3 Microservices for Notifications

For the task management app, we will add a simple **notification microservice**. This service will handle sending notifications when a task is completed or created.

Setting Up the Notification Microservice

1. Create a new directory for the notification microservice:

   bash

   ```
   mkdir task-manager-notifications
   cd task-manager-notifications
   npm init -y
   npm install express axios
   npm install --save-dev typescript
   @types/express @types/node
   ```

2. Create a `tsconfig.json` for the microservice.
3. Create the **notification service** in `src/notificationService.ts`:

   typescript

   ```
   import express, { Request, Response } from
   'express';

   const app = express();
   const port = 6000;

   app.post('/notify', (req: Request, res:
   Response) => {
     const { message } = req.body;
     console.log(`Notification sent: ${message}`);
     res.status(200).send('Notification sent');
   });
   ```

```
app.listen(port, () => {
  console.log(`Notification service running on
http://localhost:${port}`);
});
```

- The notification service exposes a simple `POST` `/notify` endpoint that logs a notification message.

15.2.4 Inter-Service Communication

The **frontend** and **backend** will communicate via HTTP requests (REST), while the **backend** and **notification service** will communicate via HTTP as well.

To integrate the notification microservice, the **backend** can call the notification service's `POST` `/notify` endpoint when a task is completed.

For example, inside the backend's `/tasks` route handler, we could trigger a notification:

typescript

```typescript
import axios from 'axios';

// Inside /tasks route handler
axios.post('http://localhost:6000/notify', {
  message: `Task ${task.name} has been completed!`,
})
  .then(() => {
    console.log('Notification sent');
  })
  .catch(error => {
    console.error('Error sending notification:',
error);
  });
```

15.3 CI/CD Pipeline, Monitoring, and Logging

In a production environment, it's crucial to have a solid **CI/CD pipeline**, **monitoring**, and **logging** to ensure smooth deployments, quick detection of issues, and proactive system maintenance.

15.3.1 Setting Up CI/CD with GitHub Actions

GitHub Actions is a popular tool for automating the CI/CD pipeline. We'll set up a simple pipeline to automate testing, building, and deploying the full-stack application.

15.3.1.1 Setting Up the Workflow

1. Create a `.github/workflows/ci.yml` file in your repository:

```yaml
name: CI/CD Pipeline

on:
  push:
    branches:
      - main

jobs:
  build:
    runs-on: ubuntu-latest
    steps:
      - name: Checkout repository
        uses: actions/checkout@v2

      - name: Set up Node.js
        uses: actions/setup-node@v2
        with:
          node-version: '14'

      - name: Install dependencies
        run: npm install
```

```yaml
    - name: Run tests
      run: npm test

    - name: Build app
      run: npm run build

    - name: Deploy to production (Optional)
      run: npm run deploy
```

- This pipeline runs on every push to the `main` branch, installing dependencies, running tests, building the app, and optionally deploying it.

15.3.2 Monitoring and Logging

Monitoring and logging are essential for tracking the health of the system in production. For logging, **Winston** or **Pino** are popular logging libraries for Node.js, while **Prometheus** or **Datadog** can be used for monitoring.

15.3.2.1 Setting Up Winston for Logging

Install **Winston** for logging:

bash

```bash
npm install winston
```

In your backend service, set up Winston for logging:

typescript

```typescript
import winston from 'winston';

const logger = winston.createLogger({
  level: 'info',
  format: winston.format.json(),
  transports: [
    new winston.transports.Console({ format:
winston.format.simple() }),
```

```
    new winston.transports.File({ filename:
'combined.log' }),
    ],
});
```

```
logger.info('Backend started');
```

15.3.2.2 Setting Up Prometheus for Monitoring

Prometheus can be used for gathering metrics from your services. You can expose a /metrics endpoint in your services, where Prometheus can scrape the metrics.

```bash
npm install prom-client
```

Create a metrics endpoint:

```typescript
import { collectDefaultMetrics, Registry } from
'prom-client';

const register = new Registry();
collectDefaultMetrics({ register });

app.get('/metrics', async (req: Request, res:
Response) => {
  res.set('Content-Type', register.contentType);
  res.end(await register.metrics());
});
```

Prometheus will then scrape the metrics from your services at regular intervals, helping you monitor the system's health in real-time.

15.4 Best Practices for Maintenance and Future Growth

Building a full-stack application is just the beginning. Maintaining and scaling the system involves regular updates, refactoring, and ensuring the system can handle increasing traffic and complexity.

15.4.1 Version Control and Continuous Deployment

Using **version control** (like **Git**) ensures that changes to the system are tracked and can be rolled back if necessary. Integrating version control with a **CI/CD pipeline** ensures that each change is automatically tested and deployed to production.

15.4.2 Refactoring for Scalability

As your application grows, refactoring will be necessary to ensure that the system remains scalable. This includes:

- Breaking down services further if needed.
- Improving database performance (e.g., indexing, query optimization).
- Ensuring that communication between services is as efficient as possible.

15.4.3 Monitoring and Alerts

Set up **alerts** in your monitoring system (like Prometheus or Datadog) to notify you when the system experiences issues, such as high CPU usage, slow response times, or database errors. This helps you respond quickly to production problems and ensure the system's stability.

Conclusion

In this chapter, we covered how to build and deploy a **full-stack TypeScript application** with the following components:

1. A **React frontend** that communicates with the backend via RESTful APIs.
2. An **Express API** that manages business logic and interacts with the frontend.
3. A **microservice** for notifications, demonstrating inter-service communication in a scalable microservice architecture.
4. Setting up **CI/CD pipelines** to automate the build, test, and deployment processes.
5. Implementing **monitoring** and **logging** to keep track of system health and diagnose issues quickly.
6. Best practices for **maintaining** and **scaling** the system as it grows.

By following these practices, you can build a robust, scalable, and maintainable application that can handle increasing traffic and complexity over time. The **hands-on project** helped you integrate all these pieces into a working full-stack app, laying the foundation for any future projects you may embark on.

www.ingramcontent.com/pod-product-compliance
Lightning Source LLC
LaVergne TN
LVHW022345060326
832902LV00022B/4254